Past Masters

General Editor Keith Thomas

Disraeli

Past Masters

John Vincent

Disraeli

Oxford   New York

OXFORD UNIVERSITY PRESS

Oxford University Press, Walton Street, Oxford OX2 6DP

Oxford New York Toronto
Delhi Bombay Calcutta Madras Karachi
Petaling Jaya Singapore Hong Kong Tokyo
Nairobi Dar es Salaam Cape Town
Melbourne Auckland

and associated companies in
Berlin Ibadan

Oxford is a trade mark of Oxford University Press

First published 1990 as an Oxford University Press paperback
Reprinted 1992

British Library Cataloguing in Publication Data
Vincent, John, 1937–
Disraeli. — (Past masters)
1. Politics. Theories of Disraeli, Benjamin. 1804–1881
I. Title II. Series
320.5'2'0924
ISBN 0-19-287681-3

Library of Congress Cataloging in Publication Data
Vincent, John Russell.
Disraeli / John Vincent.
p. cm. — (Past masters)
1. Disraeli, Benjamin, Earl of Beaconsfield, 1804–1881 — Political and social
views. 2. Disraeli, Benjamin, Earl of Beaconsfield, 1804–1881 — Religion.
3. Disraeli, Benjamin, Earl of Beaconsfield, 1804–1881 — Criticism and
interpretation.
I. Title. II. Series.
941.081'092—dc20 DA564.B3V56 1990 89–23070
ISBN 0-19-287681-3

Printed and bound in Great Britain by
Biddles Ltd, Guildford and King's Lynn

For Leo

Owing to their historical position, it became the vocation of the aristocracies of France and England to write pamphlets against modern bourgeois society. In the French revolution of 1830, and in the English reform agitation, these aristocracies again succumbed to the hateful upstart. Thenceforth, a serious political contest was altogether out of question. A literary battle alone remained possible. But even in the domain of literature the old cries of the restoration period had become impossible.

In order to arouse sympathy, the aristocracy were obliged to lose sight, apparently, of their own interests, and to formulate their indictment against the bourgeoisie in the interest of the working class alone. Thus the aristocracy took their revenge by singing lampoons on their new master, and whispering in his ears sinister prophecies of coming catastrophe.

In this way arose feudal socialism: half lamentation, half lampoon; half echo of the past, half menace of the future; at times, by its bitter, witty and incisive criticism, striking the bourgeoisie to the very heart's core; but always ludicrous in its effect, through total incapacity to comprehend the march of modern history.

The aristocracy, in order to rally the people to them, waved the proletarian alms-bag in front for a banner. But the people, so often as it joined them, saw on their hindquarters the old feudal coats of arms, and deserted with loud and irreverent laughter.

K. Marx and F. Engels, *Manifesto of the Communist Party*
(London, 1848)

Preface

The novelist who has not been revived is Disraeli. Yet, though he is not one of the great novelists, he is so alive and intelligent as to deserve permanent currency, at any rate in the trilogy *Coningsby*, *Sybil*, and *Tancred*: his own interests as expressed in these books—the interests of a supremely intelligent politician who has a sociologist's understanding of civilization and its movements—are so mature.

F. R. Leavis, *The Great Tradition* (London, 1948), 1.

To speak of Disraeli in the same breath as other 'past masters' such as Plato, Christ, and Marx may seem strange. It would certainly have amused Disraeli. More politician than man of letters, more novelist than political theorist, he was above all a courageous adventurer mainly remembered for becoming Prime Minister. Yet there are good reasons for discussing Disraeli. First, if not quite a thinker, he was intelligent about the nature of politics. Secondly, he has a scarcity value. Good political novelists are few: he almost invented the political novel. Conservative political writers are likewise thin on the ground, and those who deal with modern conditions are rarer still. Burke may tower above him, but whereas Burke was not thinking in terms of governing a modern urban population, Disraeli was.

In his belief that conservatism and modernity could be happily reconciled, Disraeli has so far been proved right. In Britain, conservatives have done well out of modernity. Disraeli is the best prophet conservatives have. Yet he is also an ironist of the first order. Together with Peacock, Wilde, and Waugh, he offers a corrosive sense of the ridiculousness of normality. In this he is far from obviously conservative. His widest appeal today, especially to those on the anti-liberal left, arises from his freedom from illusion, his contempt for the mystifications of party and Parliament, his awareness of class and class culture, and his tenacious, if hardly disinterested, assertion that liberal political ideas were a form of social control. His scepticism about the legitimacy of the British liberal state of the eighteenth and nineteenth centuries was so radical as to amount to a one-man attempt at a counter-culture. It is an open question whether Disraeli does not offer more to the modern left than to the modern right.

If Disraeli was subversive about the pieties of the British constitution, he was also a radical innovator in literature. He was not only one of the first 'social' novelists (in *Sybil*); he virtually invented the parliamentary novel. He showed, perhaps better than anyone has done since, how the novel could explore political life. Trollope, who loathed Disraeli, followed in his footsteps; but where Trollope used politics to illuminate character, Disraeli's prime purpose was to use character to explain politics. Disraeli discussed politics in four ways: in novels, in works of political theory, in public speeches, and in private letters and conversation. Each bears on the other, but by common consent the novels are pre-eminent, winning the praise of even so severe a critic as Dr Leavis.

Disraeli was neither a mere Tory tribal figure nor the narrow exponent of reactionary doctrine. His only prejudice was against narrow prejudice. He was indeed a critic of the Victorian mainstream, of secular progressivism; but to oppose orthodoxy is the obvious way for a man of ambition to make his mark, and Disraeli was as ambitious in literature as in politics.

Like most Victorian thinkers, Disraeli was a critic of liberal utilitarianism. A whole herd of independent minds took that route. Where he differed from his fellow-rebels was in turning instead not to some ethical or aesthetic doctrine, but to history, to political sociology, to the inner life of the ruling class, and to the relation between high politics, religion, and the total structure of society. No wonder that Marx still puzzles the peasantries of Eurasia with his acid gibes at 'feudal socialism', and thus by implication at Disraeli, in the *Communist Manifesto*. Both Marx and Disraeli substituted the social materialism of a historically informed sociology for abstract understandings of political life. Inside Marx was a conservative sceptic; inside Disraeli, a subversive enemy of received ideas.

Disraeli's polemical works, unlike his novels, made little mark at the time, and were confined to the first phase of his life, before he was a serious political figure. Indeed, he wrote only one work of formal political theory, his *Vindication of the English Constitution* (1835). This shows him as a pugnacious opponent of utilitarian simplicities; but others were to do that job better. After 1840 Disraeli wrote no pamphlets, no signed journalism (though he wrote anonymously on immediate issues in the 1850s), no works of theory. He did not overflow with creativity, always preferring stratagem to energy. As a parliamentary tactician, of course, he was endlessly fertile; but few things leave a less lasting mark. A biography in 1852, a novel in 1870, another novel in 1880, a fragment of a novel (about Gladstone) in 1881—and that, after his Young England trilogy of 1844–7, was all.

Disraeli is short on major output and highly patchy in quality. This does not greatly matter. At his sharpest, he fills a unique position in political criticism, in political sociology, and in political fiction.

Acknowledgements

My grateful thanks are due to Alan Bell, Librarian of Rhodes House Library, for scholarly counsel; to David Dinkin, for permission to consult his Bristol thesis on Disraeli's racial thought; to John Murray, for permission to use their new edition of *A Year at Hartlebury*; to Faber and Faber, and to Lord Quinton, for permission to cite his *The Politics of Imperfection*; to Macmillan, for use of Daniel R. Schwarz, *Disraeli's Fiction*; and to Harvester-Wheatsheaf, for permission to cite my *Disraeli, Derby, and the Conservative Party: the Stanley Journals 1849–1869*. I am grateful to Hamish Hamilton for use of H. M. and M. Swartz (eds.), *Disraeli's Reminiscences*; and to Eyre & Spottiswoode and to Lord Blake for quotations from his *Disraeli*. To M. G. Wiebe, general editor of the *Benjamin Disraeli Letters*, and the Disraeli Project, Queen's University at Kingston, Ontario, I express special thanks for timely aid.

I acknowledge gratefully the part played by Lord Blake's great biography in creating the framework of discussion; by Dr Sheila M. Smith's work on the novels; and by the stimulating additions to discussion made by Mr P. R. Ghosh and Professor Paul Smith.

To my friends at Shrewsbury I give special thanks for their help with a little-known period of Disraeli's career; and, last but never least, I pay tribute to the constructive interest of several generations of Bristol students in the interpretation of Disraeli.

Contents

Abbreviations

A	*Alroy* (Bodley Head, 1906).
B	Blake, *Disraeli* (Eyre and Spottiswoode, 1966).
C	*Coningsby* (The World's Classics; OUP 1982).
CF	*Contarini Fleming* (Hughenden edn.; Longmans, 1881).
DR	*Disraeli's Reminiscences*, ed. H. M. and M. Swartz (Macmillan, 1975).
E	*Endymion* (Hughenden edn.).
F	Sir William Fraser, Baronet, *Disraeli and his Day* (Kegan Paul, 1891).
GP	General Preface to the Novels (Longmans, 1870).
HT	*Henrietta Temple* (Panther, 1969).
L	*Lothair* (Longmans, 1870).
LGB	*Lord George Bentinck* (Routledge, 1858 edn.).
M & B	Monypenny and Buckle, *Life of Disraeli* (John Murray, 1910–20).
P	*Popanilla* (Hughenden edn.).
R	*Letters of Runnymede* (John Macrone, 1836).
S	*Sybil* (The World's Classics; OUP 1981).
Schw.	Schwarz, *Disraeli's Fiction* (Macmillan, 1979).
T	*Tancred* (Hughenden edn.).
V	*Vindication of the English Constitution* (Saunders and Otley, 1835).
VG	*Vivian Grey* (Centenary edn.; Moring, 1904).
YD	*The Young Duke* (Hughenden edn.).

1 Biography

BENJAMIN DISRAELI was born in London on 21 December 1804 into a respected and well-to-do family. His paternal grandfather, a straw-bonnet merchant from Italy, had arrived in England in 1746, and had prospered. His only son, Isaac D'Israeli (1766–1848), a Tory propagandist and religious sceptic, had never had to work, except at his chosen vocation of being a widely read writer of *belles-lettres*. An entirely urban child, Disraeli had the considerable advantage of being born and brought up in the literary section of the metropolitan upper middle class.

Things did not quite work out as they should have. Though Benjamin, the eldest child, was certainly free of provincialism, he grew up under disadvantages which he then proceeded to multiply. Unlike his two younger brothers, who went to Winchester and became conventional civil servants, he went neither to public school nor university. He left school when he was about 15, roamed his father's library, spent three doubtless formative years as a solicitor's clerk, and thereafter was not to have a paid job again until he was 48 and became Chancellor of the Exchequer. Thus at the age of 20, in 1825, he was a very ambitious youth of distinctive character, patchy education, and no prospects.

There followed perhaps the worst set-backs of his life. Between 1825 and 1830 his career collapsed. His health broke down, he became permanently indebted through rash speculations, he acquired a bad name, and he saw no one who mattered. He did nothing most of the time, except write, and what he wrote was poor stuff. At the age of 25, a literary semi-invalid pottering in the country, he must have looked a hopeless case. A long Mediterranean tour in 1830–1 restored his health, widened his horizons, and

1

increased his confidence. He returned in late 1831, having missed the chance to play reformer, but determined to cut a figure in West End society. Despite ever-pressing debts, he made headway as a raffish social climber in the years 1831 to 1836. By 1835 he had a mentor, the wily Tory Lord Chancellor Lord Lyndhurst; by 1836 he was in the Carlton Club and accepted quis a Tory.

In the late 1830s his luck turned. He married money, and got into Parliament. The money, it is true, was less than he had hoped for; the seat, Maidstone, was corrupt and served him only until 1841. The marriage was devoted and childless. Mrs Disraeli had her eccentricities—which perhaps added to Disraeli's taste for rural retirement—but nobody questioned his loyalty to her. Very likely the fact of her being older than him provided just what he most wanted and needed: a maternal figure. By the late 1830s Disraeli had retrieved some, if not all, of the disasters of his youth. He was, however, a figure of little consequence. He spoke rarely in the House. Between 1837 and 1847 he was never appointed to its committees. Until 1844, perhaps even until 1846, it is doubtful whether the average member would have heard Disraeli speak.

In his books alone he made some progress. Seen from today, his writings of the 1830s appear juvenile compared with his works from *Coningsby* (1844) onwards. But this view relies too much on hindsight. It is true that Disraeli wrote too rapidly, wrote for money, and was aiming (without success) at a best seller. But it is also true that the novel of the 1830s was an immature, half-formed thing. As a writer, Disraeli was above all a man of the 1830s; and he remained so, with little change, until his death in 1881. Byron had died in 1824. The question was what came after Byron; and until the 1840s one was not to know that the answer was the Victorian novel. The Victorians came to see Disraeli's novels as *sui generis*, not of their time; but placed against the background of the 1830s, Disraeli becomes far less untypical.

He was an ambitious young man of the 1820s, turned into a social climber and man about town of the 1830s. Thereafter he did not at heart turn into anything else—though appearances changed very much, for after 1846 he affected Victorian decorum, senatorial *gravitas*, and the ordinariness of the average country gentleman. Apart from his Mediterranean tour of 1830–1, Disraeli was content to travel little. There were business visits to Paris, writing holidays at Spa, but nothing regular, nothing that was a necessity to him. If he had a real need, it was solitude in the Chiltern woods about his house, after the parliamentary session finished in mid-August. The Mediterranean had meant much to him, but he never revisited it, remaining a Home Counties romantic. Against his father, who lived to 1848, he never rebelled, save over money. The reverse is the case. It is impossible to tell where his father's ideas end and Disraeli's begin. His father wrote voluminously and with authority on English letters and politics in the seventeenth and eighteenth centuries, a field on which Disraeli often drew. It may be suspected that Disraeli's historical disquisitions were often potted versions of the elder D'Israeli's discourses.

In the 1830s, an age of literary experiment, Disraeli was an experimentalist, trying first one genre, then another. It was impossible to see any general direction. He did not only write long-winded trash much of the time; worse, he did not know he was writing it. From this unhappy state of affairs, Young England rescued him. Young England (or 'feudal socialism' as Marx quaintly called it) was politically ineffective but of some imaginative importance. It was a tributary entering the general current of criticism of free-market liberalism. As such, it enlarged the range of what could be said, and it led Disraeli to write novels of lasting importance. *The Tragedy of Count Alarcos* (1839), a verse drama and his last work before Young England, fell dead from the press; his next work, *Coningsby* (1844), belongs to the permanent inheritance of educated men.

3

Young England, a small group of Tory back-benchers, did not originate with Disraeli. It sprang from the historical, religious, and social ideas of three young Tory MPs just down from Cambridge, who sought a livelier, less economic, less managerial version of Conservatism than Peel offered. As a group, it was short-lived. It began in late 1842, attracted notice in 1843 and 1844, and broke up amicably in 1845. Nowadays it might almost be called a dining club. Its prime rule was worldly enough: 'membership should not interfere with the taking of office'. Disraeli had his own, even worldlier, scheme: to use an expanded Young England, holding the parliamentary balance, as a secret vehicle for French policy in return for funds—a mild form of treason, in fact, though his plan came to nothing.

Disraeli, despite his intellectual borrowings from his younger friends, nevertheless had a persistent, if more prosaic, record of his own as the poor man's friend. To the Young England years of, at most, 1842–5—an apparent flash in the pan—must be added his support for the Chartists (even while opposing educational reform) in 1839 and 1840; and in 1841, before the election, he voted four times against the hated Poor Laws. Though not the most active or original member of Young England, Disraeli's record in 1839–45 did hang together coherently, even if wooing the borough mob was among his motives.

Disraeli's novels did not sell widely, despite their recognized merits. They do, however, leave us in some doubt as to whether he was aiming at political or literary fame in the years before 1846. In December 1845, indeed, we find him working as Palmerston's secret go-between in Paris, using his contacts with the King of the French. How far he was Palmerston's factotum we do not know, for the evidence has been destroyed. Still, a Tory back-bencher who works secretly for a Whig leader can hardly be thinking of his future in purely party terms.

The Corn Law crisis of 1846 transformed all this. Disraeli, probably acting as a hired gun, attacked Peel not on grounds of economics, of which Disraeli knew little, but on grounds of inconsistency and betrayal of pledges. (In 1842 Disraeli had supported Peel's tariff reforms, saying that free trade was a Tory not a Whig policy.) Disraeli's performances were masterly, and rallied an otherwise inarticulate back-bench revolt. In bringing down Peel, Disraeli did not intend that the great Tory majority of 1841 should commit suicide for a generation. On the contrary, the newly published *Disraeli Letters* reveal his plan of July 1846 for a 'Grand Junction Government', uniting all shades of Tory opinion. With an unknown peer as Premier, the real work of parliamentary management was to be left to Disraeli and Gladstone (for whom Disraeli cherished high esteem); Peel was to take a diplomatic post overseas. None of this happened. The easy passing of the Corn Law Repeal (which Disraeli did not expect) and the failure to turn a 'Peasants' Revolt' among back-benchers into tenure of office constituted a double defeat for Disraeli in 1846.

Nobody then or since disputed Disraeli's rhetorical power, small though its intellectual (as opposed to literary) content was. However, rebellion in itself did not land Disraeli the Tory leadership: far from it. Above him, but in the House of Lords, towered Lord Derby, the Olympian party leader, whose authority no Tory ever challenged. Disraeli, at best, was Lord Derby's House of Commons manager. Disraeli proposed; Derby decided. It was long indeed before Derby's relations with Disraeli were anything but frigid. Whether they were ever warm, may be doubted.

Derby apart, the Conservatives in the House of Commons found Disraeli hard to swallow. To those who wanted reunion with the Peelites, Disraeli was the hatchet that had to be buried. He embodied a disunity that many Tories wished to forget. He was personally obnoxious. But he was the only talent the Derbyite faction had; and by 1849 he was one of a triumvirate of Tory leaders in the Lower House, nominally equal, but really the only one who mattered. Leadership altered Disraeli perhaps more than marriage had done. He put

5

his pert and gaudy youth behind him. He always wore brown, a loyal follower reported, and never smiled. He overdid the gravity, as he had previously overdone the dandyism. In one particular, however, he did well: he became a convincing country gentleman, remaining so all his life.

Of course, an inveterate debtor like Disraeli could not purchase even a modest property like Hughenden, close to his former Buckinghamshire home of Bradenham. The great Tory family of Bentinck paid. Theirs was the party of the country gentleman; their leader must be a country gentleman too. And a very good artificial country gentleman he made: happily rural outside the session, a county member, a diligent county magistrate, founder of the Buckinghamshire police. This was the setting of his maturity: the long, and also lean, period when he was second-in-command of the opposition, from 1849 to 1868.

Disraeli was the greatest leader of the opposition modern Britain has known. He also led his party in opposition for longer than anyone else. Both are curious claims to fame. They reflect a simple truth: there were more Liberals than Tories. The Tories came in, and then only briefly, only when the Liberals quarrelled. Genius is a strange word to use of a man who, as a party leader, lost six general elections and won only one.

Twenty years soon goes. Disraeli had little to show for his middle age. In 1845 he was only just putting his youth behind him. In 1866, as he entered his sixties, he was contemplating retirement. His role in the party depended on Derby being in the Upper House, not on his being well-regarded by Tory opinion generally. Had Disraeli retired with Derby, as he might well have, his mark on the historical page would today be faint. For all the agility of Disraeli's parliamentary tactics, his opposition leadership lacked a theme. Mid-Victorian Toryism became a pale echo of dominant Liberalism. 'Liberal Conservative', a favourite label of the period, meant a Tory in search of Liberal votes. 'Conservative progress' became a Tory cry—but Tory progress curiously resembled Liberal progress. Where policy was concerned, Disraelian Conservatism before 1874 was open to the charges of latitudinarianism that Disraeli had made against Peel. The neo-feudalism of Young England had virtually vanished: the clock was not to be put back.

It was not to be put forward very far either. Disraelian Conservatism remained true to its birth in two respects: it was the party of the gentry, and the party of the Church of England. It was weak in Scotland, and weakening, by 1868, in Wales. It was usually weak in Ireland. It was a much more specifically English party than the Liberals. It might flirt with popular doctrines, and was not a party of resistance pure and simple; but its social character remained exclusive. Its social identity remained its leading doctrine.

If Toryism, though fully sharing in the anti-democratic consensus, had no intention of being branded as an enemy of the people over the question of electoral reform, it was partly because it had a far better issue on which to make a stand. From about 1860 the Tories, and especially Disraeli, modernized reaction by resisting aggressions upon the Church of England, an institution with a large popular base. This was a wise and, indeed, a new departure: Disraeli had not made the Church a theme in the 1850s. The more threatened the Church became, the more it needed a mass Tory party as its defender. Thus, at a time when gentry Conservatism abroad was losing its rank and file, gentry Conservatism in Britain was gaining one. Religious sectarianism, opposition to temperance fanatics, and an anti-Irish working class (Bible, beer, and brawls) were the three pillars which made realizable Disraeli's rhetoric of a popular and national party.

A 'popular and national' party was best defined by what it excluded. It was code for a gentry party which to a large extent excluded the middle class. Disraeli did not like the middle classes; he did not seek to encourage them; and he saw them, rather than the urban worker, as the enemy. The middle classes of the 1860s and 1870s were becoming reactionaries, but Liberal reactionaries; Disraeli appears not to have foreseen on any scale the growth after 1868 of late Victorian suburban and commercial Toryism. Disraeli did not prevent the growth of a mass party. He did not promote it energetically, for energy was not his style. His *métier* was parliamentary manoeuvre. In the 1850s he turned an embittered gentry splinter group into a national gentry party, without himself ever becoming a focus of emotion outside Parliament.

Disraeli's achievements can be enumerated. The government fell more often than ever before or since: 1851, 1852, 1855, 1857, 1858. The Derbyites regained control of the House of Lords. There was a slow *rapprochement* between the Court (essentially Peelite) and the Derbyites. The party organization, lost to Peel in 1846, was ably rebuilt. So were party funds: the Tories became the richer party. Another blessing was that the Tories had no leadership problem, unlike the Liberals. The party ate out of Derby's hand. In foreign policy the Derbyites were cool, calm, and collected, free from bourgeois excitement. They were especially good with Napoleon III. In successive incidents—Don Pacifico, the Papal Aggression, the Crimean War, the Indian Mutiny, the US Civil War—Disraeli in particular displayed a sanity and reticence which look well today. Since Palmerston had cornered the market in brinkmanship and chauvinism, it fell to Disraeli to embody self-restraint.

Disraeli's efforts nearly worked. In 1859 the Derbyites won their best election result between 1841 and 1874. Eight more MPs could have made them the natural governing party during the boom years of the 1860s. Once in, the payroll vote would have done the rest. Had they achieved office with a majority while Disraeli was in his prime, as so nearly happened, there was no reason why the Derbyites should not have come to look as impressively inevitable as the Gladstonian Liberals; for the new generation of militantly Christian Conservatives—Northcote, Gathorne Hardy, Salisbury, Carnarvon, Cairns—was as able as anything the other side could produce. However, the years continued to slip away. In the 1860s Disraeli took life rather more quietly, even writing (though not publishing) a fragmentary autobiography. Disraeli, like everyone else, was waiting for Palmerston to die. Instead, Palmerston only grew in popularity. An inter-party pact guaranteed the government in the early 1860s. Never before or since in peacetime has an opposition formally agreed not to oppose.

Palmerston's death in 1865 was followed by several years of parliamentary uncertainty, enhanced by economic difficulties and a radical political mood among urban workers. The ostensible issue was once again electoral reform. Disraeli's part in this was limited. If he had sublime insights, he kept them to himself. He made three proposals about reform. The first was to settle the matter without delay; the second was to do nothing; the third was to play for time by setting up a commission. All were brushed aside. Disraeli was left to execute other men's plans, and did so with such tact, lack of scruple, and open-mindedness that he kept his party in power (though in a minority of eighty), broke up the Liberals, and made himself Derby's inevitable successor when Derby suddenly fell ill in February 1868. In the process he enfranchised the urban worker, more or less, but the central intention was personal and parliamentary survival. Electoral reform, though not Disraeli's main stock in trade, had served him well. The same could not be said of religion, to which he now turned in his brief first ministry of 1868.

Disraeli had not made any platform speeches on church questions, with one minor exception, before 1860. He then began a series of regular platform appearances as 'Defender of the Faith' each year from 1860 to 1865 inclusive. In 1862 he asked: 'Is man an ape or an angel? My Lord, I am on the side of the angels.' Churchiness was Disraeli's answer to a Palmerston whose reactionary liberalism was impregnable to normal party assault. This new-found interest led to the apparently systematic political exploitation of church issues, most notably Irish Church disestablishment in 1868, the Irish university question in 1873, and the 1874 Public Worship Act. In fact, all three cases were largely fortuitous. In 1868 Disraeli had to bow to the hard right in his Cabinet; in 1873 the apple dropped into his not very expectant lap; in 1874 he took up legislation prepared by the Archbishop, and allowed himself to be swept along by a Protestant tide.

As it turned out, Disraeli's greatest asset was Gladstone. The radical wind of the late 1860s could not last forever. While it blew, Disraeli lay low. In 1871 the tide began to turn. The main issue between then and the 1874 election was an over-active, overbearing Gladstone. When the Tory leaders feebly plotted Disraeli's departure in 1872, they were already too late.

Disraeli's second ministry (1874–80) was the first Conservative government with a clear majority since Peel. It was welcomed by figures as representative of liberal tradition as Earl Russell and George Eliot. The reaction of the 1870s went deep. The mood of the times was against doing anything, and in particular against any increase in local taxation. This virtually ruled out a social programme. Disraeli still behaved as if the Conservatives were a natural minority. He wooed right-wing Whigs with Cabinet posts. He made an approach to Earl Russell. He cultivated the young Rosebery and Harcourt, both future Liberal leaders, but at this time Disraeli's young men. Oddest of all, back in 1868 when old Derby lay sick, he had offered his job to Granville, Liberal leader in the Lords. Conservatism would only flourish, Disraeli seemed to feel, when it had enough Liberals aboard.

Disraeli was an old, frequently ill Premier. As early as the autumn of 1874 it was doubtful whether his health would permit him to continue. Public pressure was for inertia; his revenues were declining after the boom year of 1874. To do anything from such a boxed-in position would have been remarkable. At first, in 1874, 1875, and 1876, Disraeli did nothing in particular and did it moderately well. He kept the Commons happy, and avoided large political issues.

He kept his party together. He let his ministers, mostly able men, run a government of departments. He misjudged public opinion on several occasions: over Scottish Church patronage, over escaped slaves, over Plimsoll and the safety of merchant shipping. Perhaps, too, the Royal Titles Act of 1876 which made Queen Victoria Empress of India was an error of judgement, for it startled rather than impressed, and reminded a staid public of his supposed taste for gaudiness. In retrospect, but in retrospect only, the social reforms of 1875 stand out. They did not so stand out at the time. They were seen more as an absence of conventional politics than as a policy that defined a party. They should not be linked with the troubled 'conscience of the rich' that marked the 1880s. Still, more social legislation was passed in 1875 than in many a year before or since. Since little of it was controversial, it fulfilled Disraeli's election pledge of 1874 for quieter times and less energy in domestic affairs.

The question is what kind of legislation. Much was not compulsory: as Disraeli said, 'permissive legislation is the characteristic of a free people'. Local authorities were empowered to take action on certain issues, an unlikely prospect given ratepayer resistance. Central government, wherever possible, passed responsibility to the localities. The Public Health Act of 1875, often listed as a reform, was a consolidation act: essentially a reprint. The Artisans' Dwellings Act, not widely adopted, was the last of the mid-Victorian public health reforms rather than the first step towards council estates. The Merchant Shipping Acts, it was said, required a Plimsoll line, but allowed owners to decide its location—around the funnel, if they wished. The Food and Drugs Act allowed town councils of grocers to crack down on the grocery trade at their discretion. More substantial was the trade-union legislation, taken over from Liberal measures found in the pipeline. A Cabinet with little knowledge of industry legalized picketing and breaches of contract by strikers, doing so with a broad brush when something more rigorous was required. Disraeli's motive was partly electoral.

11

The bills, he said, would 'gain and retain for the Conservatives the lasting affection of the working classes'. The Prime Minister fell asleep as they went through Cabinet: the first time he had ever done so.

All this, except at the level of broad strategy and parliamentary helmsmanship, had little directly to do with Disraeli. The minister chiefly responsible was Sir Richard Cross, the Home Secretary, squeezed into the Cabinet by Derby, a Rugby and Lancashire friend. Disraeli's test of success was keeping the Liberals down; and indeed the opposition did not really recover until 1879. With Gladstone in retirement from 1875, Disraeli excelled in the small detail natural to quiet times.

Had Turkey, the 'sick man of Europe', not chosen this moment to collapse in bankruptcy and Balkan uprisings, the Disraeli ministry might well have run its course without any major event. But bankruptcy and uprisings were not enough by themselves to make 'the Eastern question' come alive in domestic politics. The Bulgarian atrocities of May 1876 changed all that. Disraeli had no responsibility for these local massacres by Turkish irregulars: it was Gladstone who, to save money, had abolished our men on the spot. Disraeli was responsible, however, for some light-hearted parliamentary replies which exasperated high-minded opinion. With the August temperature in the nineties, provincial Britain became explosive, stirred up by a coalition of churchmen, dons, and journalists.

With the agitation fully established, Gladstone now jumped aboard. His famous pamphlet, *Bulgarian Horrors and the Question of the East*, sold 200,000 copies. It made any defence of Turkish integrity hopeless. But it made the question political, and soon Disraeli felt the solid ground of patriotism under his feet. Since 1870 Disraeli had made the Liberals look left-wing and anti-patriotic: the theme used by Palmerston against Cobden. Disraeli's role model after 1870, indeed, was Palmerston, much more than Derby. The Tories, he asserted, put British interests first, and that meant opposing the Russian bear. On this level, the Eastern question was a way of splitting the Liberals once again, as in 1866–7. It worked: in 1877–8 the Liberals were very split indeed. The Bulgarian atrocities campaign, superficially a great radical moment, established Disraeli's credentials as national leader as nothing else had.

But there was more to it than dismantling the opposition. Disraeli had his own views. To keep the Cabinet together he had to be conventionally anti-Russian and pro-Turkish, for that was what the party and the public expected; but on his own account he was looking for plunder. Disraeli was no innocent Turcophile. The only part of the Empire that held any interest for him was India. The thought of founding another India in the Middle East was one of his motives in 1876–8. He cast a covetous eye on Constantinople. He acquired Cyprus. He set up a system of military consuls in Asia Minor. It was not an empire; but it was how empires start.

Disraeli, by 1878, represented consensus. The British public feared war with honour, for which they were militarily ill-prepared; peace with honour, with some apparent gains in prestige, suited John Bull's taste for victory on the cheap. In practical, or Balkan, terms, Disraeli's 'peace with honour' was not territorially very different from Gladstone's 'bag and baggage' policy. The choice facing the British public was between two styles: high-mindedness versus national prestige.

From 1878 Disraeli was at last master of his party, even a venerated figure. This was a new development. The question is whether anti-Semitism stood in his way, or whether his character and conduct created anti-Semitism. There are isolated examples of what people really thought. In 1859 a Tory grandee wrote to Derby complaining of 'that nasty, oily, slimy Jew'; Derby read the passage with great glee to those at White's Club. The Duchess of Buccleuch, the greatest Tory lady, thought in 1867 that 'we can never have a united party as long as Dizzy is the head of it'. The same year, an eminent back-bencher groaned: 'That hellish Jew has got us in his power.' (In electoral terms, Tory anti-Semitism had very little discernible effect. At Shrewsbury in 1841, for example, Disraeli finished a mere ten votes behind one Gentile running-mate; and in Buckinghamshire in 1874 he was one hundred votes ahead of another.)

Liberal anti-Semitism was more overt, more respectable, and more important. Trollope made a system of ethics out of condemnation of Disraeli's unmanly, or Jewish, qualities. Robert Browning wrote: 'We don't want to fight, but by Jingo if we do, the head I'd like to punch, is Beaconsfield the Jew.' Leading academics like the historian Freeman revelled in anti-Semitic innuendo. The Liberal anti-Semitism of the 1870s led easily into the progressive, anti-imperialist anti-Semitism of the Boer War period.

After the glamour and tension of the Eastern question (1876–8), 1879 was everything a Prime Minister dreads: a slump, record unemployment, agricultural depression, defeat in Zululand, massacre in Kabul, even endless rain at harvest. With revenues reduced and taxes rising, the government could neither contemplate a social programme nor take credit for social reforms already achieved. Disraeli had nothing to offer at the 1880 election except a scare on the Home Rule issue. He may have been prescient; the public was uninterested. The Liberals exploited an infallible mixture of moral indignation and financial irritation, against a setting of bad trade. As an example of the mindlessness of popular politics, it could hardly be bettered. To Disraeli, it was but one more turn of fortune's wheel. He took a seven-year lease on a Curzon Street house: no question of retirement there. His health was hardly worse than in 1874. He began a new novel, never completed, called *Falconet*, whose hero was a fictional version of Gladstone. Had Disraeli lived long enough to see Liberalism destroyed by Ireland, as he foresaw in 1880, what polished unity writers would have given to his career! As it was, he died on 19 April 1881, almost incidentally, the result of going out on a cold night.

Lord Randolph Churchill's lapidary verdict was 'Failure, failure, failure, partial success, renewed failure, ultimate and complete victory.' Thus it seemed to the Tory young of 1880, anxious for a romantic hero. (Could Derby, could Peel, ever have given rise to the Tory rank-and-file cult of the Primrose League, so called after Disraeli's favourite flower, which was widely worn on the anniversary of his death?) Party wishful thinking apart, where does Disraeli stand?

Outside the House of Commons, he was no political genius. He did not judge the popular mood well, nor did he show much electioneering instinct. He kept his party together: the Harold Wilson of Conservatism. His tact as a parliamentary manager was extraordinary; but persuasion was not leadership, for he held office chiefly when the country was in torpid moods which required him to suppress his greatest quality—agility. Perhaps, too, he failed the greatest test. He lanced no boil, as De Gaulle did with Algeria, and Margaret Thatcher with organized labour. His traditionalism was marked. He preserved the stable rural identity of Derbyite Conservatism. He left his party untransformed. His innovations concerned slogans not social identity, and the slogans were of the reactionary centre. He wrapped the Tories in the Union Jack. He inherited Palmerston's mantle. He had some progressive policies, but he avoided dwelling on them. Far more important than social reform in his rhetoric was his idea of the innate solidarity of the English people behind their natural leaders. 'One nation', as handled by Disraeli, was no more a code for social or political progressivism than it was the war-cry of a party of resistance.

'One nation' was the celebration of shared experience within a happy family. Disraeli adapted traditional Conservative political theory, especially Burke's and Coleridge's rejection of Benthamite rationalism, to urban industrial conditions, which he saw as propitious to Conservatism. As Lord Quinton says: 'Disraeli had seen the emergence of

15

class conflict into the centre of public political consciousness as an unhappy aberration, a pathological but curable
condition of a fundamentally healthy organism.' Enemies
there were—Dissenters, Irish, Scots—but their enmity only
cemented English unity. Disraeli is a rare specimen of a
Conservative social optimist, too sceptical to feel threatened or fearful as Liberal reactionaries genuinely did. His
scepticism and endless plasticity of purpose were concealed
beneath a fake *gravitas*, an exaggerated pose of normality: he
bore out his own maxim, 'The British People being subject
to fogs and possessing a powerful Middle Class require grave
statesmen.' Praise him we may for courage, resource, and
invention; but can we ever know a Disraeli who is more
than the sum of his enforced poses?

2 Disraeli's Political Theory

THOUGH born into a Tory household, the young Disraeli had no very definite political line. His absence abroad in 1830–1 prevented him from climbing aboard the Whig and reforming bandwagon, even if he had wanted to and the Whigs had been prepared to accept him. By 1832 he was belatedly searching for a political place of abode. It was not easy. 'I am neither Whig nor Tory. My politics are described by one word, and that word is England', he wrote in *Gallomania* (1832), an attack on the government's foreign policy. 'Toryism is worn out, and I cannot condescend to be a Whig', he told a friend in June 1832. It is not enough to say that until 1835 Disraeli was willing to stand under almost any banner, and to seek votes from almost any quarter—though he was. It was his rationalization of his tactics that mattered and was to prove enduring. As his biographers say: 'even in 1832 all the elements of his finished political creed can already be detected' (M & B i. 229). Certain traits stand out. Disraeli was never a narrow radical partisan. The destructive left had no charm for him; was he not the heir to a Buckinghamshire squire, with an inheritance to lose? He was never a Whig. He always sought a broad and popular base on which authority and stability might be restored. In that sense only was he a democrat: he wished to achieve conservative objects by modern means.

His pamphlet *What Is He?* (1833) presented a choice: revert to aristocracy, or advance to democracy. 'I feel it absolutely necessary to advance to the new or the democratic principle.' Even though the Reform Act was, in its detail, 'so essentially aristocratic', the 'aristocratic principle has been destroyed in this country, not by the Reform Act, but by the means by which the Reform Act was passed'. If the Tories accepted this, it was 'their duty to coalesce with the Radicals' and form a national party. By 1834, in another pamphlet, *The Crisis Examined*, Disraeli's call was for 'a National Administration and a Patriotic House of Commons'. That, no doubt, meant a House with him in it; but it also meant getting rid of the obsolete mental furniture of British *ancien régime* politics. Each man has his formative decade, and whereas in literary and moral outlook Disraeli was a young man of the Byronic 1820s, in politics he was a young man formed by the experience of the 1830s.

Disraeli wrote only one work of political theory, his *Vindication of the English Constitution* (1835). He never attempted such a work again, preferring fiction, biography, and polemic. Yet he was not negligible as a political theorist, for he combined two elements in the *Vindication*: his own theory, based on inferences from English history, as to the nature of political society; and a criticism, essentially correct, of utilitarianism. Within one cover he sought to say both what the world was like and what it was not like.

He first defined as his enemy the 'anti-constitutional writers' who sought to submit all institutions 'to the test of UTILITY, and to form a new constitution on the abstract principles of theoretic science'. Utility, he objects, is a term without meaning. Or rather, because it can mean anything, it means nothing. The utility of a material object may be known; but there is no test of moral and political utility except the various opinions of mankind. Utility, says Disraeli, is what you think it is; it is unverifiable, and therefore of no use as a touchstone. As for the utilitarian slogan, 'the greatest happiness of the greatest number', the same applied. Such a formula was equally compatible with despotism, gross superstition, a military empire, or with a free republic. Who, in any case, was to judge what constituted the greatest happiness? Utility, in short, was a mere phrase, capable of serving any interest or emotion. As a test, it was, or ought to be, politically neutral: neither radical nor conservative. Yet, in practice, utilitarians thought ill of the world and sought its reform. Here they relied on a false doctrine of human nature, namely self-interest. The slogan, for such it was, would serve if it were defined as the infinite variety of motives that influence men. But the Utilitarian party of Disraeli's day admitted not all, but only some forms of self-interest: desire for power, and desire for property. From this false psychology, their other falsehoods followed.

Armed with this over-simple view of human nature, the utilitarians attacked privilege—monarchy and aristocracy not least. Because man by their definition was selfish, monarchy and aristocracy must represent the highest form of selfishness. Their remedy was to replace both by entrusting government to the people, meaning in effect the middle class. 'To say that when a man acts, he acts from self-interest, is only to announce, that when a man does act, he acts.' (*V* 13.) 'Utility, Power, Pain, Pleasure, Happiness, Self-interest, are all phrases to which any man may annex any meaning he pleases'—and from which anyone could produce any political theory they happened to require. Indeed, it was a fallacy to think that 'theories produce circumstances, whereas circumstances indeed produce theories' (*V* 15). Disraeli's complaint against utilitarianism was not just that it was epistemologically weak and logically superficial. It was that, like all non-historical and abstract theories, it did not grow out of the past experience of mankind. The utilitarian error was to found institutions on theories, 'instead of permitting them to be created by the course of events, and to be naturally created by the necessities of nations'. Theory overlooked the ruling passion in an individual, and was thus bad psychology; it overlooked national character, and was thus, in modern parlance, bad sociology.

Here Disraeli stood, in his historical materialism, at the point at which Burke met Marx in a common scepticism about historical abstractions. Conscious no doubt that philosophy was hardly his strong point, whereas he had an inherited taste for history, Disraeli made history the basis of his thought. He was a natural plagiarist. Whether he knowingly plagiarized Burke, or (excusably) wrote in his shadow, matters little. But when he said that 'the foundation of Civil Polity is Convention' (*V* 23); that society was an 'artificial creation' to which all owe a debt (*V* 25); that 'a most salutary legal flavour' pervaded our history; and spoke admiringly of the school who 'looked upon the nation as a family, and upon the country as a landed inheritance' (*V* 24), his affiliations were clear enough.

How far did Disraeli's criticisms of the utilitarianism of his day hit the nail on the head? In the first place, he was right that utility is indeed a politically neutral criterion; only by historical accident had it become a radical war-cry. (In a later generation, the great Lord Salisbury was to be both a utilitarian and a keeper of the Conservative conscience.) Secondly, he was right to stress the epistemological snags: how was one to know what was useful, and who was to be the judge? Thirdly, he was unusual (and right) in challenging the narrowness of contemporary English psychology and sociology. A nascent radical democracy was no more likely to maximize happiness than a well-run absolutist state like Prussia, or a decadent hedonistic empire like Turkey. This was (and is) well worth pointing out, especially to English audiences. Fourthly, Disraeli, unlike most Victorian literary opponents of utilitarianism, damned it not for its aridity and lack of soul, but on sceptical grounds. Most anti-utilitarians objected to it because they believed life had a higher meaning; Disraeli's objection was that abstract words, divorced from history, had no meaning: 'Utility, Power, Pain, Pleasure, Happiness, Self-interest, are all phrases to which any man may annex any meaning he pleases.'

Had Disraeli had the stamina, the cultural background, or the motive to write more than the fifteen or so pages of philosophical analysis in the *Vindication*, he might have made an interesting philosopher of the extreme nominalist or reductionist type. As it was, he lacked all these things— especially the stamina. However, he said just enough, by way of prologue, to establish why, for his purposes, the only true thought was historical thought, either expressed in a combative general sociology (as in the later part of the *Vindication*) or as exemplified in fiction. Disraeli's literary practice and his scanty theory go hand in hand—just.

History did not mean to Disraeli what one might have expected. Was he not, after all, the son of a subtle, voluminous, and informed Tory historian; the loyal heir of Burke; and the pupil of Lord Lyndhurst, the wily Tory Lord Chancellor to whom the *Vindication* was dedicated? Yet Disraeli's view of English history is as much Whig history as that of Hallam or Macaulay. He wrote palpable, crass, unblushing, philistine, optimistic, evolutionary Whig history; and having written it, he ingeniously turned it to Tory ends. England, the 'most flourishing society of modern ages', had 'for many centuries, . . . made a progressive advance in the acquisition of freedom, wealth, and glory' (*V* 3–4). No nation could lay claim to 'superior learning or superior wisdom; to a more renowned skill in arts or arms; to a profounder scientific spirit; to a more refined or comprehensive civilisation' (*V* 25–6). Britain, indeed, was the 'ornament and honour of the world'.

Britain's greatness was rooted in freedom, and its freedom in history. The English were 'universally held to be the freest people in Europe, and to have enjoyed our degree of freedom for a longer period than any existing state' (*V* 25). The credit belonged to the men of 1688, who 'had secured nearly a century and a half of the greatest order, prosperity, and glory, that this country, or any other country, ever enjoyed' (*V* 45). The Stuart case, so ably stated by Disraeli's father, was brushed aside. Divine right was dismissed as a 'fatal superstition'; the reigns of the later Stuarts were 'the most disgraceful in our annals' (*V* 124). We are urged to look instead to 'our wise ancestors, in a political sense, since the Reformation': Henry VIII, Burleigh, Cecil, Walsingham, Coke, Selden, Strafford, Pym, Cromwell, Clarendon, Sir William Temple, William III, Lord Somers, Marlborough, Argyll, Walpole, Bolingbroke, Mansfield, Hardwicke, and

Burke, men who, whatever their party, 'invariably agreed' to 'eschew abstractions' (*V* 62).

In true Whig manner, Disraeli traced the growth of liberty back to its remote beginnings. 'The Declaration of Right connected the pedigree of our rights and liberties with the Petition of Right, which again carried them upwards to the great Charter, in like manner dependent on the charter of Henry Beauclerk, and the Laws of the Confessor.' (*V* 43.) Magna Carta was a 'blessed deed' which should command 'reverential gratitude' as the 'broad foundation of our national liberties', giving 'an equality of civil rights to all classes of English freemen'. By the fifteenth century, indeed, the 'present Constitution of England was amply, if not perfectly, developed' (*V* 88).

This picture of English liberties broadening down from precedent to precedent had long been suspect to scholars (as Disraeli must have known), and was long to be acceptable to John Bull. Disraeli's exaggerated praise for the 'august and admirable fabric' of the British constitution was partly meant to serve the immediate polemical purpose of confounding the radical reformers of the 1830s. But it had a more strategic purpose: to break the supposed links between freedom and progressivism, freedom and democracy. Whig history, he was to show, could serve Tory ends.

On one level, the object of Disraeli's Tory scepticism was to demystify. In this he resembled the sceptical side of Marx. Where Marx saw democracy as the fig-leaf of capitalism, Disraeli saw 'progressive' politics (whether revolutionary, majoritarian, or democratic) as not what the people do, but what is done to the people by politicians. Behind the participatory slogan lies the manipulative and élitist reality: here Disraeli anticipates the iron law of oligarchy. Disraeli went out of his way to accept the Whig heritage of freedom and prosperity. It was only the Whig party he wished to discredit as narrow, sectarian, élitist, and corrupt. This was no small task. Had not the Whig party made England both great and free? So said received opinion. The Tories of 1832 had come to swallow the Whig myth, and to see themselves as a thin blue line holding back the forces of anarchy. Disraeli's polemical genius was to reverse the argument: to show the Whigs as the oppressive few, the Tories as the oppressed many, and the so-called 'forces of anarchy' as none other than John Bull—moral, conservative, patriotic, and deferential. Disraeli stood the anti-majoritarianism of post-French Revolution Toryism on its head, redefining the many throughout English history as sound fellows, and the Whig few as the true enemies of Whig freedom and the Whig popular heritage. This was contrived. It swam with the Whig tide of the day, yet made the Whig party into everybody's enemy. It was a doctrine designed to mop up diffuse discontents of left and right. Yet for all its short-term cleverness, in the bad sense, it was not necessarily untrue. Walpole's England may have been a Whig republic with a latent Tory majority. The Whig grandees of Holland House who presided over Britain in the 1830s were an exotic cultural and family cousinhood, not the people.

Disraeli's *Vindication* of 1835 foreshadowed his Young England novels of the 1840s, his party leadership, and his premiership. He had learned the lesson of 1832: that there was no longer a place for a party of resistance. True, there was as yet, in 1835, no mention of social questions; but subject to that exception, Disraeli had learned a clever trick which he never forgot. Faced with an established Whig supremacy both in his parliamentary constituency and in literature, he retorted with an anti-élitist or popular doctrine of national solidarity: 'trust the people' was code for 'distrust the Whigs'.

Outflanking was nothing new in politics: James II had tried it. Outflanking in a modern context was. Disraeli's sincerity may be untestable, his political practice erratic, but his consistent awareness of the emotional unity of right and left was neither. He was the Tory practitioner most aware of the scope offered by a mass line. Since politics is inherently oligarchical, most must suffer from a sense of exclusion. Bring that sense to life, and you have a natural majority. 'The Tory party is the national party; it is the really democratic party of England', he argued. To the Tory of 1835 this would have been a paradox indeed. Democracy was then, and remained for long afterwards, a word that sent a shiver down the spines of those with anything to lose. Even in the eighteenth century, he continued, 'nine-tenths of the people of England formed the Tory party', made up of 'the landed proprietors and peasantry of the Kingdom, headed by a spirited and popular Church' (*V* 80).

Why, then, had the Whigs held sway? They were 'not a national party', but 'a small knot of great families who have no object but their own aggrandizement, and who seek to gratify it by all possible means' (*V* 172). They sought to reduce the Crown to a 'Venetian Doge' (*V* 139, 168, 177). Worst of all, by 1835 they had become an 'anti-national party', dependent on Scottish and Irish votes, but lacking a natural majority in England. As for Whig policy, it was a loud hypocrisy. By civil and religious freedom, the great Whig slogan, they meant a doge and no bishops; 'advocating the liberty of the subject, the Peers would have established an oligarchy; upholding toleration, the Puritans aimed at supremacy. This is the origin of the Whig party in our country.' (*V* 176.) The seventeenth century also showed the Tories as the party of the many, resisting the tyranny of a clique. The key to the Civil War, the last baronial revolt, was the sudden rise of a King's party from nothing, and the tender attachment of the people to Anglicanism; whereas the Long Parliament was a dreadful warning of the dangers of revolutionary oligarchy.

Disraeli's version of British history lurched wildly between the fanciful and the penetrating. There was indeed habitual exaggeration of language and tone. But the surprise today is how incisive he was on central issues, and how his absurdities related chiefly to minor points. There is another point to consider: his writings of the 1830s and 1840s were those of a man who did not know which side would win, yet wished to be on the winning side. By identifying oligarchy as the central tune of British history since the Reformation, he left it open whether to hop nimbly into the embrace of Crown and gentry should reaction triumph, or to lead the popular cause if revolution came. To have two sets of credentials made good sense for a young man starting out in the 1830s.

If the *Vindication* was intended to show Disraeli's capacity for philosophic seriousness, the *Letters of Runnymede*, also published in 1836, more than made up for this by displaying party spirit in its crudest form. In a series of letters dedicated to Peel, the Tory leader whom Disraeli was to destroy ten years later, Disraeli proclaimed that the Tories were winning the intellectual battle in splitting the Whigs from 'the people'. Perhaps they were. The Whigs had had a bad session, and the Tory opposition was on its way back. But Disraeli's case lost credibility from its straining after effect. In one passage he compared one minister to an ape, another to a cat, two more to 'sleek and long-tailed rats', the Lord Chancellor to an onion or a cheese, O'Connell to a crocodile, and Lord John Russell to an insect (*R* 64). When Disraeli stooped, he stooped very low.

The *Letters* were meant to be 'illustrative of Whigs and Whiggism' by displaying 'the essential and permanent spirit of the party' as exhibited down the centuries. In this they failed. Disraeli's political arguments were wooden until he put them into fictional form. Personal abuse of opponents, hatred of the Irish, and a portrayal of party politics as numbers versus property, ignorance versus knowledge, dissenting sects versus established institutions, in no way did justice to his intelligence. His flattery of Peel knew no bounds: Peel's ministry of 1834–5 was 'your brief but masterly premiership' (*R* 39); Peel now stood as 'the head of the most powerful and the most united opposition that ever mustered' (*R* 13). He admired in Peel 'that devotion to your country which is your great characteristic' (*R* 37); 'in your chivalry alone is our hope' (*R* 36). 'What a contrast

25

does your administration as Prime Minister afford to that of one of your recent predecessors! No selfish views, no family aggrandizement, no family jobs, no nepotism'. (*R* 38.) 'Pitt himself, in the plenitude of his power, never enjoyed more cordial confidence than that which is now extended you.' (*R* 39.)

Such views had much to commend them. Disraeli in the mid-1830s was the self-appointed laureate of Peel's centrist, modernizing latitudinarianism: an intelligent swimmer with the tide, not a neo-feudal ideologist longing to put the clock back.

3 Disraeli as Racial Thinker

DISRAELI was a racial thinker. He thought race 'the key of history' (E 248). 'All is race', he wrote (LGB 239); 'All is race; there is no other truth', said Sidonia (T 149). Race, for him, transcended everything: it explained religion; it explained politics. Disraeli was far more of a racial than a social or religious thinker. And very conveniently, race justified Disraeli, a converted middle-class Jew, taking his place among the Tory aristocracy on equal terms.

Disraeli's racial doctrine went the whole hog. Not only was race the key to history, but some races were far superior to others. There were master races, and there were the rest. Their superiority was a biological matter rather than just a cultural one, and depended on purity of blood. Interbreeding caused racial degeneration. If such doctrines ring oddly today, let us recall that they were advanced for the best of reasons: to raise a downtrodden people, the Jews, in the esteem of mankind, and to raise them, moreover, not to equality, but to a position of hardly undeserved superiority among the nations. Disraeli was unusual not because he used the common coin of pseudo-scientific racial thought, but because he used it for Jewish (and therefore, in the circumstances, virtuous) ends. Disraeli said little about the lower races; his object was to praise, not to disparage. There was an absence of malign intent. Still, Disraeli believed that to think racially was to be modern and scientific. As he wrote in 1870 in the General Preface to his novels: 'the great truths of ethnology' taught that 'race implies difference, difference implies superiority, and superiority leads to predominance'; the implication being that these were truths but recently arrived at.

Of Disraeli's sincerity and consistency, at least, there can be no doubt. His view of race remained constant in the

27

novels, from *Coningsby* in 1844 to *Endymion* in 1880; and what he said in the novels coincided with what he wrote in the solemn pages of the biography of his dead friend, Lord George Bentinck. Both biography and novels again tallied with his speeches in Parliament on Jewish disabilities, his private letters to a Jewish lady, and reports of his private conversation. There can be no question of his interest in race, during the last forty years of his life, being a literary affectation: *Alroy*, *Coningsby*, *Tancred*, and *Endymion*, among the novels; the debates of 1847; the biography of Bentinck; his private letters, his reminiscences, his reported conversations, and his preface to his father's works—all pointed to the same conclusion.

When Gentiles were concerned, Disraeli did not elaborate upon his ideas very much. In *Endymion*, for instance, he divided Europe into Teutons, Slavs, and Celts. Elsewhere, he added the Semitic peoples, Arab and Jew, to the list of Caucasians: a most unorthodox classification. 'The Arabian tribes rank in the first and superior classes together, among others, with the Saxon and the Greek . . . The Mosaic Arabs are the most ancient, if not the only, unmixed blood that dwells in cities.' It was the Semitic race alone that seriously concerned him. If the Semites as a whole were superior, the Jews were the élite of the Semites. Between Jews and Arabs, Disraeli made little or no distinction; Arabs, he said, were 'only Jews on horseback'. Christ was 'a man of Arab blood'; the Rothschilds were 'like an Arabian tribe' (*DR* 19) in their family feeling. The Jews were 'a Bedoueen Race' with 'beautiful Arabian traditions' (*T* 346, 352). Because of 'the unpolluted current of their Caucasian structure', the Jews retained 'the primeval vigour of the pure Asian breed' (*C* 193).

The great virtue of the Semites was their purity of blood. 'The decay of a race is an inevitable necessity, unless it lives in deserts and never mixes its blood.' Indeed, 'you cannot destroy a pure race of the Caucasian organisation. It is a physiological fact: a simple law of nature.'(*C* 218–19.)

The impure races, including most European peoples, would simply vanish into the dustbin of history. As Sidonia tells Coningsby: 'You must study physiology, my dear child. Pure races of Caucasus may be persecuted, but they cannot be despised, except by ... some mongrel breed ... itself exterminated without persecution, by that irresistible law of Nature which is fatal to curs.' (*C* 221.) Deserts had enforced racial purity on the Arabs; persecution had done as much for the Jews. Only the Jews 'could claim a distinction which the Saxon and the Greek and the rest of the Caucasian nations have forfeited. The Hebrew is an unmixed race.'

The races of northern Europe were not only racially impure; they were, partly in consequence, vulgarly materialistic. They were a 'society which has mistaken comfort for civilisation'. 'God has never spoken to a European', Tancred learned; 'God never spoke except to an Arab'. To commune with deity, 'a qualification of blood as well as of locality' was required; 'the favoured votary must not only kneel in the Holy Land but be of the Holy Race'. For the 'mongrel breeds' of Christian Europe, half-pagan by comparison with the Semitic nations, the outlook was bleak. 'The mixed persecuting races disappear; the pure persecuted race remains.'

Such strong meat could not be offered to English readers without making them a special exception to the sorry tale of European miscegenation. English superiority, Disraeli claimed, was 'an affair of race. A Saxon race, protected by an insular position, has stamped its diligent and methodic character on the country.' Disraeli explained the tensions of his own day as a conflict between lordly Norman and native Saxon (echoing Scott's *Ivanhoe*): 'The Norman element in our population wanes; the influence of the Saxon population is felt everywhere, and everywhere their characteristics appear. Hence the honour to industry, the love of toil, the love of money, the love of peace, the passion for religious missions, the hatred of the Pope, the aversion to capital

punishments . . .' (*LGB* 239.) In practice, Disraeli said as
little as was decently possible about the merits of the Anglo-
Saxon race; his heart clearly was not in it. His object was
to celebrate the Semitic races, their unique place in human
history and religion, and, since he was a great believer in
secret societies, their role as the greatest secret society of
all. Such evidence as he drew from his own times was
remarkably inaccurate, but he believed deeply in Jewish
centrality: 'The Semites are unquestionably a great race,
for they invented our alphabet. But the Semites now exercise a vast influence over affairs by their smallest though
most peculiar family, the Jews. There is no race gifted with
so much tenacity, and such skill in organisation.' The Jews
might look powerless, even crushed; but to the initiated
they were a great force, a hidden hand. 'As you advance
in life, and get experience in affairs, the Jews will cross
you everywhere.' (*E* 249.) Though 'all the tendencies of the
Jewish race are conservative', persecution caused 'men of
Jewish race to be found at the head' of 'the secret societies
who form provisional governments'. 'The people of God
co-operate with atheists; the most skilful accumulators of
property ally themselves with communists . . .' (*LGB* 357).
This doctrine was to have a sinister history in the century
ahead.

Disraeli came close to the idea of a Jewish world conspiracy
or network, managed by a master race defined by purity of
blood. 'Language and religion do not make a race—there is
only one thing which makes a race, and that is blood.' (*E*
249.) Philo-Semitism could be strangely like anti-Semitism:
pseudo-scientific, cranky, and bothered about interbreeding
(for example, when Disraeli argued that if white Americans
were to mingle with Blacks, 'they would become so deterio-
rated that their states would probably be reconquered and
regained by the aborigines . . .'). 'Blood', to Disraeli, was
biological; nature, not nurture. Thus he repeatedly claimed
for Jews 'a peculiar musical talent, an almost exclusive privilege of music' (*C* 222). 'Musical Europe is ours . . . Almost

every great composer, skilled musician, almost every voice that ravishes you ... springs from our tribes', he wrote in *Coningsby*; wild talk indeed.

Why did Disraeli lay such stress on race? Politically it did him little good. As a matter of prudence he would have done better to keep quiet about his Jewish convictions. It was a sad case of a man of the world being overcome by sincerity. Had he not believed in race to some extent, it would have been odd; the idea was common currency among men of his day. It served, among other things, to signify nationality, tradition, culture: prosaic elements in any historical analysis. To believe in the Jewish race, and to say so, loudly and repeatedly, in a Tory and Anglican context was, however, bizarre.

We can only guess at his motives. Dinkin, the chief authority on his racial views, suggests that Disraeli's philo-Semitism was a retort to anti-Semitism encountered in youth and early life. This is certainly possible; but Disraeli himself did not suggest it in his autobiography, for instance; and the novels made no overt mention of anti-Semitism in an English context. Going further back, Disraeli also failed to make anything out of the burning and torture by the Inquisition of his paternal grandfather's parents-in-law by his first marriage (from which Disraeli was not descended). So little is known of Disraeli's youth that any interpretation must be highly speculative; but his undoubted early sense of isolation, like his many set-backs, may have owed more to his being Disraeli than to his being a Jew.

Alternative views are at least conceivable. In the 1840s Disraeli entered the Rothschild orbit. For a novice politician with chronic debts, nothing could look more promising than to set up as Rothschild's bulldog. In *Coningsby* Rothschild appeared as the Jewish superman; he was still appearing in *Endymion* (1880) as the all-wise spider at the centre of the web. If, to be crude, Rothschild (Disraeli's executor) bankrolled Disraeli, or if Disraeli hoped he would, then he certainly got good value.

31

A quite different possibility is that Disraeli was engaging in a party manoeuvre. He had done much for the protectionists in 1846; but they were determined to do little for him in 1847–8. Perhaps he wanted Liberal credentials, and a *casus belli* for breaking with his party. Perhaps, too, he looked for employment from Palmerston (an embassy, perhaps?) in return for having been his political factotum in the mid-1840s. (*Tancred* described Palmerston as greater than the elder Pitt.) Tory leaders are not often agents for Liberal Foreign Secretaries, which is maybe why the evidence has again disappeared. But there was certainly a secret connection, and in 1855 Palmerston proposed Disraeli for the Istanbul embassy.

These explanations are not mutually exclusive. A hard core of visionary sincerity was also involved, of a proto-Zionist kind. Talking to a close political disciple, young Lord Stanley, in 1851, Disraeli spoke, with a seriousness and intensity quite contrary to his normal manner, of restoring the Jews to their native land. He gave details, down to the probable split between eastern and western Jews which would result (and has resulted), showing how fully he had thought over the matter; and declared with un-Disraelian passion that the man who fulfilled these hopes 'would be the next Messiah, the true Saviour of his people'. Perhaps no less significant was his intention that, on retirement, he would write a life of Christ from the Jewish national point of view, for posthumous publication.

Because Disraeli had no Boswell, we can never fully grasp his Jewish dimension, something he could never share with Gentiles. It was probably more intense and more central than we shall ever know. One fact alone we can be sure of: it developed gradually, quite late in life. As he wrote to a Jewish widow in Torquay who left him £40,000: 'I, like you, was not bred among my race, and was nurtured in great prejudice against them. Thought, and the mysterious sympathy of organization, have led me to adopt the views with respect to them, which I have advocated and which

... have affected in their favour public opinion.' Disraeli's assertion of Jewish racial superiority jumped the gun. Except in finance, the Jews were neither flourishing nor particularly important in the 1840s, Disraeli's most Jewish decade; the Jews of Palestine, whom Disraeli had seen in 1831, were in an especially wretched state. To make his case, Disraeli had wildly to exaggerate Jewish achievement; Mozart, for instance, he claimed as a Jew. The astonishing flowering of the Jewish mind in science, culture, and philosophy that was to occur around the turn of the century still lay far ahead. In retrospect, but in retrospect only, Disraeli's more absurdly inflated claims have come to look like uncanny prescience. More haunting is another reflection: 'The world has by this time discovered that it is impossible to destroy the Jews. The attempt to extirpate them has been made under the most favourable auspices and on the largest scale ... A superior race shall never be destroyed or absorbed by an inferior ...'

This vision of Jewish indestructibility merged into Disraeli's commitment to the aristocratic creed. As Sidonia says in *Coningsby*: 'an unmixed race of first-rate organisation are the aristocracy of nature' (*C* 192). Disraeli, as a natural aristocrat, thus rationalized his place in an aristocratic party. (He even believed, quite wrongly, that he was of aristocratic descent in Jewish terms.) He also rationalized the connection between English Toryism and the spiritual values of Palestine by striking an anti-Western, anti-Enlightenment pose. 'Enlightened Europe is not happy. Its existence is a fever, which it calls progress. Progress to what?' So far as this was not literary concoction, it was based on Disraeli's keen contempt for the fussy, ephemeral, and pretentious nature of secular liberalism.

Disraeli's racial theory was something of a curate's egg. Some of its main components—purity of blood, racial superiority—are not exactly in vogue. Such underpinning of fact as Disraeli deployed (for example, the dominance of music by Jews) was quite unreliable. Of his continued conviction that the 'general influence of race on human action [was]

33

universally recognised as the key of history' (GP 13–14), there can be no doubt. Behind the nonsense, lies a noble and generous attempt to do justice to a great but oppressed people, in terms acceptable to the English Anglican mind:

For myself, I look upon the Church as the only Jewish institution that remains . . . and must ever cling to it as the only visible means which embalms the memory of my race, their deeds and thoughts, and connects their blood with the origin of things.

There are few great things left, and the Church is one. No doubt its position at the moment is critical . . . but I believe the state of affairs is only one of the periodical revolts of the Northern races against semitic truth, influenced by mortifying vanity at never having been in direct contact with the Almighty . . .

This was a literary vein to be worked; a winning position to be occupied; but it represented also a consistent loyalty which Disraeli always claimed to be one of his main qualities.

Those who react strongly against Disraeli's racial views should perhaps ask themselves if they would have thought better of him had he remained silent and not sought, by the means afforded by the culture of the day, to vindicate the Jewish people. They should also consider some points in his defence. First, Disraeli disliked racial cranks: Aryan ones. In *Lothair* he mercilessly derided Mr Phoebus and his pseudo-racial 'Aryan principles' which involved the idolatrous worship of nature and art instead of the Semitic truths of Arabia. Nature and art, like science, were false gods; whereas it was 'the intellect of Arabia that comes from the Most High'. In his novelist's way, Disraeli was distinguishing between race as a basis for traditional monotheism, and race as a pseudo-basis for contemporary fashion and its restless search for epiphanies.

Secondly, there was a multiracial commitment behind Disraeli's racial thought. He disliked nationalism. He feared its destructive force. He refused to meet Garibaldi. He much preferred the great multiracial empires like Austria and Turkey: he knew that if they went, somebody would get hurt; and history has not proved him wrong. Nationality is almost race; it left Disraeli cold. The power to unite the destiny of Arab and Jew in a single vision was also evident when it came to race: his practical views tended to a magnanimous coexistence of peoples. (Had he not been almost alone in not succumbing to hatred during the Indian Mutiny?) Disraeli's ideas, however odd, did not presage the racial state.

To Disraeli, race was not an end in itself. Here he differed root and branch from future racial thinkers. Race existed to provide a complete scheme of existence: broadly, ethical monotheism. (Disraeli said nothing that excluded Islam.) Was it not 'ordained that the inspired Hebrew mind should mould and govern the world?' (*T* 427.) His prescription had a social content, and a conservative one at that. For all its vague deism, was not 'the sublime and solacing doctrine of theocratic equality' laid down in *Tancred* something of a euphemism for an ordered inequality? If race underlay religion and politics, it did not, for Disraeli, replace or subsume them. *Tancred*, Disraeli's favourite novel, abounded in Jewish triumphalism. He called it 'a vindication and I hope a complete one of the race from which we . . . spring'. This reflected Disraeli's intentions, but little else. Readers were not interested; and the parliamentary controversy about Jewish disabilities did not arise until well after the book was written. Disraeli, exalted at having just destroyed the strongest government of modern times, decided to mount a full-scale attack; for *Tancred* is no meek apology for his race.

Race, and racial superiority, were at the heart of Disraeli's concept of Jewishness—religion being present but subordinate. The Hebrews are a 'miracle'; 'alone of the ancient races', they remain 'a memorial of the mysterious and mighty past'. 'Is it a miracle that Jehovah should guard his people? And can he guard them better than by endowing them with facilities superior to those among those whom they dwell?' (*T* 192.) This superiority is seen in Sidonia, the *éminence*

35

grise of *Coningsby*; in Besso, the Sidonia of the East; and in Besso's daughter Eva, who is no mean polemicist: 'We agree that half Christendom worships a Jewess, the other half a Jew. Which do you think should be the superior race, the worshipped or the worshippers?', she asks a bemused Tancred.

These might be just fictional flourishes, had not Disraeli recycled substantial parts of Eva's arguments, especially those concerning Jewish sufferings being a punishment for deicide, in his biography of Lord George Bentinck four years later. As it is, Eva stands conventional Christian anti-Semitism on its head: 'Persecute us! Why if you believed what you profess, you should kneel to us! You raise statues to the hero who saves a country. We have saved the human race, and you persecute us for doing it.' (*T* 195.) As for the ideal of integration (on Gentile terms), Disraeli exploded at the liberal notion that Jews might eventually hope to pass unnoticed: 'Consummation of the destiny of the favourite people of the Creator of the universe!' (*T* 388.)

Disraeli believed both that Jews had a finger in every pie, and that they were truly a persecuted people. 'The life and property of the people of England are protected by the laws of Sinai. . . . And yet they persecute the Jews, and hold up to odium the race to whom they are indebted . . .!' (*T* 265.) Not all Jews were as fortunate as Sidonia:

Conceive a being born and bred in the Judenstrasse of Hamburg or Frankfort, or rather in the purlieus of our Houndsditch or Minories, born to hereditary insult, without any education, apparently without a circumstance that can develop the slightest taste, or cherish the least sentiment for the beautiful, living amid fogs and filth, never treated with kindness, seldom with justice, occupied with the meanest, if not the vilest, toil, bargaining for frippery, speculating in usury, existing for ever under the concurrent influence of degrading causes which would have worn out, long ago, any race that was not of the unmixed blood of Caucasus, and did not adhere to the laws of Moses: conceive such a being, an object to you of prejudice, dislike, disgust, perhaps hatred. (*T* 389.)

Such a being, Disraeli adds, is through his faith and traditions filled with images of beauty, joy, and reverence, even of hope, embodied in prayers and ceremonies of Eucharistic grace, 'as if he were in the pleasant villages of Galilee'.

One must accept Lord Blake's view that Disraeli's racial ideas, if given credence today, would be 'at best a piece of anthropological nonsense, at worst a cause of and precedent for the anti-Semitism which he most deplored' (B 209). But though the ideas are mostly not admirable, it was admirable that Disraeli should have put them forward: admirable that he should have used his great talents as an advocate to forward Jewish emancipation; and a great act of imagination to have given a Hebrew interpretation of the history of the world.

4 Disraeli: Christian or Jew?

'I AM the blank page between the Old Testament and the New.' Thus, perhaps apocryphally, Disraeli described his religious position. In reality, no such simple phrase is adequate. Disraeli thought much about religion; he thought it mattered. His own library was limited to theology, the classics, and history; he sold his father's great collection of literature. He was a serious, even a pious, Victorian figure. He was not, however, a conventional Christian—but he was a practising one. He went to church. He took Communion. He was at pains that he, his wife, and their Jewish benefactress should receive Anglican burial together. Nearing death, he spoke of Christ and of Redemption. He was, on his mother's side, the third of his line to be buried in a church. He did not regard such decencies lightly. His enemies, had they been able, would not have scrupled to taunt him with agnosticism or religious indifference. He gave them no grounds for doing so. 'An absolute reticence as to his personal religion was one of Beaconsfield's marked characteristics', wrote his official biographers (M & B vi. 560).

Yet Disraeli held no less than four religious positions, more or less concurrently. First, he rejected conventional supernatural Christianity. Secondly, he believed that modern thought might give Christianity a deeper meaning; so he rejected conventional materialism. Thirdly, he believed in the Jewishness of Christianity. Fourthly, he believed in the social necessity of religion. Of his scepticism there is little overt evidence. His father was indifferent in religious matters; his mother was hostile to Judaism. His conversion, at 13, was an empty formality, the result of family rows and his grandfather's death. Perhaps it was a bruising experience. At any rate, it did not involve attachment to Anglicanism, for after baptism Disraeli was moved from a broadly

Nonconformist school to a Unitarian one. If anything in his youthful experience propelled Disraeli towards Anglicanism, it was this unhappy brush with dissent. Disraeli's dislike of Dissenters was lifelong and deep. The circles in which he moved in early manhood were not noted for their godliness. Morality was not smart, and smartness was for a time Disraeli's highest aim. Religious reflection, we can probably assume, belongs mainly to Disraeli's life after 1840.

Though the wider Victorian public could regard him as a church-going Anglican squire, intimates might see things differently. His disciple Lord Stanley wrote in his diary on 30 November 1861: 'how can I reconcile his open ridicule, in private, of all religions, with his preaching up of a new church-and-state agitation?' Ten years earlier the same disciple had noted in January 1851:

whether in town or country, politics constitute his chief, almost his sole, pleasure. One other topic is a favourite: the philosophical discussion of religious questions: I mean by this the origin of the various beliefs which have governed mankind, their changes at different epochs, and those still to come. This was common ground to us both; of the new German school of theology I had perhaps read more than my friend, but his acquaintance with the earlier phases of the great controversy much exceeded mine. Often and often were these matters discussed between us: so far as historical criticism is concerned we had both reached the same result, but there our agreement ended. He seemed to think that the sentiment, or instinct, of religion, would by degrees, though slowly, vanish as knowledge became more widely spread ... Yet Disraeli is no materialist: he has always avowed his expectation of some form of future existence, though whether accompanied with any consciousness of personal identity with the self of this present life, he thought it impossible to foresee. He told me that Bulwer Lytton and he had frequently conversed on these subjects.

Disraeli, then, was a modern in religion; he accepted that the familiar beliefs of folk Christianity would never pass muster again. One passage, but one only, in *Endymion*, was often taken by late Victorians as the keynote of a socially

39

respectable agnosticism: '"Sensible men are all of the same religion." "And pray, what is that?" "Sensible men never tell."' Apart from that, Disraeli left hints in his reminiscences, which were unpublished and probably written for private amusement, of his religious tendencies. One passage in particular (*DR* 103) confirms his historical attitude to religion:

Assuming that the popular idea of inspiration be abandoned, and the difference between sacred and profane history relinquished, what would be the position of the Hebrew race in universal History, viewed with reference to their influence on Man?

I thought of advertising through a medium that would command confidence £500—or even a £1,000 for the best essay on this question. . . . The Judges, perhaps, to be Gladstone, Canon Stanley, and myself. Not bound however to award the prize unless satisfied with the performance.

The choice of judges may smack of tongue in cheek; but one cannot know. Anything is possible from one who, in 1851, had talked of devoting his retirement to writing a life of Christ from the Jewish point of view.

In discussion among equals Disraeli took the believer's part: but it was belief modernized. In one case he crossed swords with Sir George Lewis, a leading Whig and 'thorough sceptical speculator'. Lewis thought that the merits of the Lord's Prayer were exaggerated. 'I thought the Lord's Prayer a masterpiece', Disraeli retorted. 'It was the most perfect exponent of the purest religious feeling, that had yet appeared.' (*DR* 102.) Another companion was always saying: 'what did Jesus do before he was thirty? My conviction is, that he must have had an eventful youth, and travelled a great deal.' 'I never could agree with him', noted Disraeli. 'It seemed such an original mind; so completely formed in seclusion, and with all its Shakespearean genius, so essentially local. All the illustrations are drawn from inward resources, or from surrounding scenery.' (*DR* 8.)

These accounts, surviving by chance alone, show Disraeli in the part of the ponderous, naïve, solemn Victorian

Christian: equipped, at the least, to talk religion at the dinner-table or on the front bench. By chance, too, we see him revising Christianity to make it believable: 'Anthropomorphism: a great cry against it by the Philosopher. But if the Hegelian principle be true, that Man is the first organisation in which God is conscious, then the old legend of Genesis, that God made Man in his own image, comes to the same thing.' (*DR* 103.) Disraeli, we may presume, did not travel far down this road of a Hegelian reconstruction of Christianity; but nor, at that date, did anyone else. In any case, even if he had found the philosopher's stone that made religion true in modern terms, it would have been politically impossible to say so. The singular thing is that Disraeli should even have been talking Hegelian religion in the early 1860s.

Disraeli admired the Enlightenment tradition of anti-Christian speculation going back to Bayle: 'Bayle is a great bank to draw upon, especially when others do not keep accounts there.' Yet its aridity led him to see it as part of the utilitarian desert, which he rejected. Too sceptical to swallow the creed of disbelief, he turned to religion as displayed in the history of his people. 'The History of the Jews is development or it is nothing. If ever a history were a history of development, it is that of the Jews.' (*DR* 104.) His Jewish view of history confirmed him in his Anglicanism:

I look upon the Church as the only Jewish Institution remaining. I know no other. A vulgar error to consider circumcision one. That marks them out only in Europe, and not in every part of Europe. If it were not for the Church, I don't see why the Jews should be known. The Church was founded by Jews, and has been faithful to its origin. It secures their history and their literature being known to all Xdom. Every day the Church publicly reads its history, and keeps alive the memory of its public characters; and has diffused its poetry throughout the world. The Jews owe everything to the Church, and are fools to oppose it. (*DR* 103.)

To Disraeli, Christianity, 'the most important portion of the Jewish religion' (*LGB* 363), was a matter of 'the Semitic principle and its most glorious offspring the Jewish faith [i.e.

Christianity]' (*LGB* 364). Such terminology would hardly conciliate.

Lord George Bentinck (1852) was a parliamentary narrative of the three years from 1846 to 1848: a matter of sugar bills and railway bills. Into this, as chapter 24, Disraeli intruded a polemical essay on the Jewish question. In literary terms, it was uncalled-for; indeed, it eschewed all mention of the parliamentary debates on Jewish disabilities. It was polemic, and it came from the heart: that, perhaps, was the difficulty. It was also over-intellectual, un-English, and braggart in tone. It made debating points, and good ones, but without tact. It expounded Christian truth and mixed it with wildly inaccurate assertions of Jewish racial superiority and political centrality. Was Disraeli, some may well have asked, the man to ascend a Christian pulpit?

Let us take Disraeli's argument bit by bit. Jews, he says, are 'the human family that has contributed most to human happiness' (*LGB* 346); Christ is 'the eternal glory of the Jewish race' (*LGB* 364); all Gentiles daily accept that 'the only medium of communication between the Creator and themselves is the Jewish race' (*LGB* 346); 'No one has ever been permitted to write under the inspiration of the Holy Spirit, except a Jew' (*LGB* 348). However true all this might be, the manner in which it was stated was hardly likely to endear the Jews to the English reader of 1851.

The argument that the dispersion of the Jews was a penalty for deicide, he dismissed as historically untrue and dogmatically unsound. Historically, the Jews had already been widely dispersed before the Incarnation; dogmatically, the purpose of the Incarnation 'was not to teach, but to expiate' (*LGB* 349). There cannot be two moralities; 'how could the Second Person of the Trinity reveal teachings not known to the First Person?' (*LGB* 350.)

Disraeli's Christianity centred upon the Atonement, a thoroughly Jewish idea, and one pre-ordained: 'If the Jews had not prevailed upon the Romans to crucify our Lord, what would have become of the Atonement? But the human mind cannot contemplate the idea that the most important deed of time could depend upon human will. . . . Could that be a crime which secured for all mankind eternal joy . . .?' (*LGB* 350.) Having scaled the heights of theology, not without success, Disraeli then turned to the social prejudice against Jews, talking much hot air in the process.

Like Matthew Arnold, Disraeli compared Hebrew and Hellene: 'the other degraded races wear out and disappear; the Jew remains, as determined, as expert, as persevering, as full of resource and resolution as ever' (*LGB* 352). 'The Greek . . . appears exhausted. The creative genius of Israel never shone so bright.' (*LGB* 354.) 'There is no race . . . that so much delights, and fascinates, and elevates, and ennobles Europe, as the Jewish.' (*LGB* 353.) Their religion ensured their morality: 'a Jew is never seen upon the scaffold, unless it be at an *auto da fé*' (*LGB* 352). It is to music that Disraeli turns to prove his point about Jewish creativity:

Were it not for music . . . the beautiful is dead. Music seems to be the only means of creating the beautiful, in which we not only equal, but . . . greatly excel the ancients. The music of modern Europe ranks with the transcendent creations of human genius: the poetry, the statues, the temples, of Greece. . . . And who are the great composers? They are the descendants of those Arabian tribes who conquered Canaan, and who by favour of the Most High have done more with less means even than the Athenians. (*LGB* 353.)

This was enough to start Disraeli on his hobby-horse of racial superiority, and hence of innate aristocracy:

The Jews represent the Semitic principle; all that is spiritual in our nature . . . They are a living and most striking evidence of the falsity of that pernicious doctrine of modern times—the natural equality of man. . . . The native tendency of the Jewish race . . . is against the doctrine of the equality of man. . . . All the tendencies of the Jewish race are conservative. Their bias is to religion, property, and natural aristocracy . . . (*LGB* 356).

In another wild flight of fancy, Disraeli claimed that persecution had made these natural conservatives into men of the left. In the 1848 Revolutions, 'men of Jewish race' were to be found 'at the head' of every one of 'the secret societies who form provisional governments', all because 'they wish to destroy that ungrateful Christendom . . . whose tyranny they can no longer endure'. Had it not been for the Jews, revolution would not have ravaged Europe. But 'the teeming resources of the children of Israel maintained for a long time the unnecessary and useless pattern': look at the revolutionary juntas, and you 'will recognise everywhere the Jewish element'.

What have we here? The Jews are behind the right, behind the left, control diplomacy, have enormous resources, occupy the key positions. Disraeli's advocacy was the stuff of which paranoid anti-Semitism was to be made. Did Disraeli perhaps foresee the horrors of the next century? Lacking the 'recognition of religious truth by the state', he predicted that after 'a period of atheistic anarchy', Europeans would return to 'the old national idolatries, modified and mythically dressed up according to the spirit of the age' (*LGB* 365). Here the Third Reich, anti-Christian and anti-Jewish, casts its shadow. As Chesterton said, post-Christian man would not believe in nothing: he would believe in anything.

Disraeli grew up in a family and a climate of ideas where the differences between Judaism and Anglicanism did not seem all that important. Theologically, the Enlightenment stressed what each had in common: a rational monotheism. In practice, the line between the two religions was surprisingly blurred. Disraeli's parents never became Anglicans, but they were buried in Bradenham Church; a maternal grandmother who regarded Judaism as a misfortune lay in Willesden Church. Yet the Disraeli children were named in accordance with Hebrew custom, and a younger brother who died in infancy was buried in accordance with Hebrew rites. Isaac D'Israeli was a man of substance, a squire living in a manor-house (from 1829). He had an honorary doctorate from Oxford, the home of Anglican exclusiveness; he even had a butler. With so philosophic a father, so at ease in the world, Disraeli was profoundly unconcerned with the

Judaic apparatus of dietary laws, sabbaths, and synagogues. In Lord Blake's judgement, 'Disraeli was surprisingly ignorant of Jewish observances, and seems to have had very vague notions about the content of Judaism' (B 503). The Judaism in which he found genuine pride and inspiration was that encapsulated in the Bible and Prayer Book. In private, he saw unconverted Jews as 'fools'; in public, as unfortunates, destined perhaps to die out as the bracing stimulus of persecution waned. 'It is no doubt to be deplored that several millions of the Jewish Race should persist in believing only a part of their religion.' (*LGB* 358.) Judaism was important, as leading to Anglicanism; but for Christ, 'the Jews would have been comparatively unknown, or known only as a high Oriental caste which had lost its country' (*LGB* 363). Disraeli was a Christian of peculiar perspective, not an apologist for Judaism.

5 Disraeli as Practical Politician

DISRAELI the writer and Disraeli the practising politician are intimately linked. 'We govern men with words', Disraeli had once written—with words, and phrases, and a political culture which makes those in authority look right, and those opposing them look wrong. Disraeli's genius was to see that you can only fight one political culture with another. By the end of his career he had established that Liberal political culture, at its best so ruggedly independent, at its worst so smugly self-approving and moralistic, could be made to look seriously wrong. He fought the battle almost alone. His colleagues, the Victorian Tories, were a dull lot; sturdy party warriors perhaps, but not capable of challenging Liberal moral certainty. (Salisbury was the exception; but he, unlike Disraeli, hardly addressed himself to the nation.) Disraeli alone had the literary creativity which lies at the heart of politics.

In practical terms Disraeli stood boxed in on every side. In economic and social matters, free-trade liberalism ruled supreme. It had produced the most successful society the world had ever seen—so Tories as much as Liberals believed. To Victorian Tories, business profits were as sacred as agricultural rents. From the 1850s onwards they supported the capitalist market economy from unshakeable and profound belief, not as a tactical concession to modernity. Had Disraeli wished to wave the collectivist flag, he would have run into insurmountable obstacles. Had he challenged those obstacles with an appeal to the people, there is no reason to suppose that the people would have responded. But, in fact, there is little evidence to suggest that Disraeli disliked market economics; which is, of course, a very different thing from saying that he shared its idolatrous worship by the Liberals.

Disraeli was against utilitarianism as a theory; but he was much more against utilitarians as people, as sad cases of misplaced seriousness. Yet, if anything, he shared their economics, as passages in *Popanilla, Coningsby,* and *Sybil* suggest, and he distrusted the hired defenders of protectionism, as the low character of Mr Toad in *Vivian Grey* indicated. In 1846 Disraeli had attacked Peel, as he later acknowledged, without saying one word in favour of protection; it was, he is reported as saying, the only way open to him, a man without means, of advancing himself. In 1841 he had steered clear of any pledge on corn with masterly ambiguity. In the 1847 election he was careful not to commit himself to bring back the Corn Laws. Much more indicative was his hard struggle—some of the hardest work he ever did—to induce the Derbyite Conservatives to abandon protection (1849–52), and to seek instead financial relief in the form of lower rates and taxes on land.

Disraeli could not, and probably did not want to, challenge the Victorian economic consensus. He was not the manor-house pink of later collectivist myth. Because he could not act distinctively in the economic area, his efforts were deflected to two more productive themes: national identity, and religion. Religion was an each-way bet. On the one hand, if Gladstone were to depart reasonably soon, and the Liberals, like the French radicals, then played the aggressively anti-clerical card, Disraeli had laid the ground for his party to be the recognized champions of Christianity. Since Gladstone not only did not depart, but served notice of eviction on Whig indifferentism and radical secularism in the Home Rule crisis, the Tories ended with a useful fallback position as the Church of England party: not the party of a natural majority, but at least the party of a bloc vote.

There were no natural majorities around to be had. The Tories were the defenders of rural interests in an ever more predominantly urban society. They were the defenders of a religious bloc which represented about half of all church-goers and much less of all adults. There were, whatever cards one played, more Liberals than Tories. The Tories won only four out of twenty elections between 1832 and 1918. There was no Tory majority between the elections of 1841 and 1874. Between 1841 and 1895 the Tories gained office only when the Liberals fell out among themselves. Even in 1874 the electorate was voting against Gladstone, not for Disraeli: it was another Liberal family quarrel. There were just not enough Tories. 'Practical politics', as the term is usually understood, could not remedy matters. Disraeli might nobble the Catholic Irish vote (as in 1859); play, the Orange card (as in 1868 and 1880); enlist the services of the publicans, threatened by Liberal temperance activists (as from 1872); or detach small groups of Liberal dissidents (as in 1866). All these were done; all were worth doing; but they could only be of limited benefit, were likely to be ephemeral, and had to be measured against long-term adverse demographic changes and the spread of radical political consciousness into new areas and lower social levels. 'Practical politics' was not the answer: the solution was to change the political culture.

There are those who hold that national identity matters little; that it is an optional extra, a cosmetic affair. The gap between the subscribers to this belief and those who consider that what holds a nation together is of the essence, is wide indeed. Those who see national identity as an extra tend to a profoundly civilian view of history which skips from one peacetime to the next; they neglect the long time-span it may require to build such national unity as Britain showed in two world wars. Be that as it may, Disraeli was boxed in as much in foreign as in domestic policy. There was no room at all for a grand new departure by a Britain which, in military terms, had decided firmly against being a great power. For that reason, Gladstonian liberalism was an intelligent way of making the best of a weak international position. Disraeli's foreign policy pretended the weak position did not exist. For the illusion of morality it substituted the illusion of strength.

One should therefore stress what Disraeli could not do, not what he might have done. His job was one in which it was impossible to succeed, except in the very long term and in a way more literary than governmental. It is just possible to argue that chance could have tipped the scales: another ten MPs in the 1852 election, an acceptance of office by Derby when offered it in 1855, another eight MPs in 1859—would these really have made the difference for long? No; Disraeli destroyed the only chance of Tory supremacy in the Victorian period when he destroyed Peel. After that, in an intrinsically Liberal world, all that could be done was to create—slowly and not without charlatanism—a counter-culture to the Liberal monopoly of wisdom. Why then did Disraeli become *the* Conservative hero?

The answer is that the choice was made early on, in the 1880s, and once having been made, it was hardly possible to say that the choice was wrong. Disraeli happened to die at a time when Conservatives badly needed a hero. His lieutenants were uninspiring. The official leaders, Northcote and Salisbury, had little public standing. The rising star of the party, Lord Randolph Churchill, drew the crowds; but some wondered if he was a Tory at all, and others if he was mad. No wonder that Disraeli never looked so good as he did in the years just after his death.

Other reasons operated to assist the process of deification. The climate of electioneering changed suddenly in the period just after Disraeli's death in 1881. The Corrupt Practices Act of 1883 came down heavily on beer, brawls, bribery, and bands. The Reform Acts of 1885 upset old ways. Politicians, unable to corrupt, had to find simple ideas and simple cults to stir the voters. The political parties began to operate publication departments on a vast scale. They began to depend much more on women and on the social side of politics, exemplified above all in the Primrose League built round the cult of Disraeli.

Again, why Disraeli? It was a question of elimination. Peel, the obvious candidate, was impossible, as a traitor to the party; Wellington's civilian career had been unfortunate; Liverpool was seen, to use Disraeli's phrase, as an arch-mediocrity; and Derby, a Whig of 1832, suffered from the disadvantage that no one knew anything about him. That left the younger Pitt, who was more Whig than Tory, and more pure minister than either. Disraeli, therefore, had to become in death a cult figure such as he had never been in his life. The practice of wearing a primrose on the anniversary of his death, a common sight in English streets until Edwardian times, was one of the most curious and synthetic of all our political traditions, and no other Prime Minister has inspired a similar rite. Indeed, only two other national figures, Guy Fawkes and Charles I (not, for instance, Nelson or Welling-ton), have entered the calendar in this way.

If the choice of party hero were made today, the answer might very well not be Disraeli. The Conservatives love success, and Disraeli's record in losing six general elections and winning only one (1874) is uniquely bad. The prize might go instead to Salisbury, for statecraft; to Balfour, for far-sighted intellect; to Baldwin, for creating social peace; to Bonar Law, for integrity; or to Churchill, for power of will. And while the choice has widened, Disraeli's standing has declined. In important senses he was not a political genius. He was not good at prediction. He was not good at handling public opinion. He was sometimes outstandingly persuasive in Parliament and Cabinet, but at other times he was capable of great insensitivity. He spent much of his life scheming, but hardly one of his schemes materialized. He searched restlessly for allies outside his own party, but never secured them. He spoke frequently outside Parliament, but built up no great oratorical reputation. Despite great efforts to merge into the background, he remained an exotic figure in British public life.

His predictions were unfortunate. He forecast disaster in the Crimean War, and was surprised by Russian defeat. He forecast success in the 1857 election, and lost heavily. He forecast victory in the 1868 election—and unwisely went round saying so—and landslide defeat followed. He thought Gladstone's Irish Universities Bill of 1873 was unexceptionable. He did not seem to expect the victory of 1874 or a major defeat in 1880. This is not to say that a politician should be judged by his skill as a psephologist, only that he should have some idea of which way the wind is blowing. And that Disraeli seems rather to have lacked.

Much the same can be said of his handling of public opinion. To take only his period of greatest success in the 1870s: Disraeli showed imagination in sketching out broad policies of 'empire' and national prestige which looked backwards to Palmerstonianism far more than they looked forward to late Victorian imperial expansion. But he had narrow ground on which to manœuvre; the public may have rejoiced in the 'peace with honour' which he brought back from Berlin in 1878, but only a small section of the population was really ready for 'war with honour'. The idea of war as a cleansing spiritual force, common in 1914, was not something to rely on in the 1870s. To the voters, however, Disraeli's discovery of 'empire' (which tended to mean prestige in Europe) only mattered at moments of unusual excitement. The voter, then as now, was a lilliputian being, concerned mainly with lilliputian issues. Of these, the most important concerned the Nonconformist vote. This had fallen away from the official Liberals in the early 1870s, in quarrels over the place of the Church in education. It was this Liberal schism, rather than Tory exertions, which returned Disraeli to power in 1874 with a large majority. Disraeli's business should have been to keep the Liberal rank and file disunited. Instead, he allowed a series of measures—on burials, education, and Scottish patronage—which had the effect of emphasizing the conflict between Anglican Toryism and Nonconformist Liberalism.

His failure in this respect is the more surprising, as splitting the Liberal ranks in the Commons was his greatest achievement. (His oratorical efforts against Peel are of less significance: first, because they did not stop Peel repealing the Corn Laws—a point of some importance; secondly, because far from removing Peel from the scene, he was left holding the balance of power in British politics; and thirdly, because it brought Disraeli little immediate benefit to be seen as the main obstacle to Conservative reunion.) In 1867 and 1877 Disraeli showed something like genius in reducing the Liberals to their constituent atoms, an achievement that was even more noteworthy because in 1866 and 1876 the Liberal impetus had seemed unstoppable and the Tory position hopeless. Disraeli's handling of the Second Reform Act and of the Eastern question only make sense in terms of the injuries inflicted on the opposition in the House of Commons.

Disraeli retained in government the opposition mentality he had learned in decades of adversity. He was not personally associated with any great measure of legislation, except for the Second Reform Bill, whose contents were not of his framing. Of his measures of the 1870s, only the dog tax, the Vivisection Act, and graduated income tax survived into the 1980s. He was Chancellor of the Exchequer three times, yet neither as Chancellor nor as Prime Minister did his budgets make a mark. In this he was simply unlucky. In a boom whoever is Chancellor appears a success; in a slump nobody does. Disraeli's luck with the economy was damnable. In 1852, working with out-of-date figures, Disraeli's budget fell apart from apparent lack of revenue; in spring 1853, with Gladstone in office and a new set of figures to hand, it turned out that there was ample money for a popular budget. In the period of Gladstone's second chancellorship (1859–66) there was an almost unbroken boom, ended, practically in the very month that Disraeli returned to the Exchequer, by a dramatic crash and serious depression. The same unhappy coincidence occurred in the 1870s. Gladstone enjoyed the last surge of mid-Victorian expansion (1870–3), using it to cut taxes to the bone; Disraeli, taking office in 1874, found himself inheriting a worsening economy, with declining revenues, nothing left to cut, and no question of spending anything on a social programme. By 1879 Disraeli was facing a major economic crisis such as Gladstone had never had to encounter. If Disraeli had had the booms and Gladstone the slumps, then Victorian politics would have looked very different.

There was another budgetary difficulty—namely, Lord Derby, who had the last word and who put the needs of defence before the needs of Disraeli. In 1852, in 1858–9, and in 1867 naval rearmament, with Derby's support, eroded all chance of a spectacular give-away budget. Again, this was a matter of chance.

On social questions Disraeli is sometimes made to appear advanced simply because comparisons are not made with the actions of other leading Conservatives in the same period. In fact, Disraeli was less actively concerned with social policy than most of his colleagues were. Even his famous slogan, 'Sanitas sanitatum omnia sanitas', was stolen, magpie-like, from an obscure French grammarian of the seventeenth century. He was content, indeed, that others should exert themselves; his own attitudes were passive and literary rather than philanthropic or political. Among his colleagues, Lord Derby (the Premier) set up a welfare state for his estate employees, and headed the relief operations in the Lancashire cotton famine of the 1860s. The younger Derby built public libraries and public baths, and ran the Peabody buildings trust. Sir Stafford Northcote was a great promoter of boys' reformatories. Sir John Pakington was a keen educational reformer. Cairns, the hard-headed Belfast man who was Disraeli's Lord Chancellor, taught in Sunday school. It is difficult to find a Conservative who was not more active than Disraeli in some form of voluntary social work. For all his general kindliness of tone towards the indigent, Disraeli was simply not a very active man outside his ordinary parliamentary routine.

There was, it is true, an *annus mirabilis* of Conservative social reform in 1875, at least in terms of legislation added to the statute-book, though little enough of what was passed (and is now conscientiously regurgitated in examinations and political speeches) made any practical difference. Some of the legislation was simply a matter of consolidating existing laws, as with the Public Health Act. Most of it was permissive, leaving it to local authorities to choose whether to take any action. Very little of it involved the spending of Exchequer funds. The legislation of the 1870s was not a move towards a collectivist state, though it was to some extent a move in the direction of collectivist local government. In any case, it is difficult to show that Disraeli himself was much involved in the details of the programme of legislation for 1875, as he was ill for a long period in the autumn of 1874 when it was being prepared. The Home Secretary, Sir Richard Cross, had been squeezed into the Cabinet at Derby's insistence, rather against Disraeli's wishes; yet it was Cross who did most of the legislative work. It is difficult to blame Disraeli personally for the fact that domestic legislation faded out after 1875, or for the awkward point that his most effective long-term measure was to give trade unions an undefined and effectively unlimited right of picketing. However, when we stress that Disraeli was no legislator, we must remember that it is the job of Conservative leaders *not* to legislate (indeed, Disraeli had come in on just such a promise in the 1874 election). One must not judge Conservative leaders by Liberal criteria. Perhaps it was the 1870 Education Act, passed with vital support from Tory votes, which should be seen as Disraeli's great collectivist achievement—and one which skilfully enforced and developed Church of England supremacy in primary education.

Foreign policy was a field in which Disraeli both did well and little. He did well because he avoided disasters, restored British prestige, and achieved a domestic triumph. He did little because there was little he could do. The question was how England could have any significance in Europe. Before 1870 there were two ways of doing this: an alliance with France to keep Russia in check in the East; or an alliance against France to keep France in check on the Rhine and in Italy. In each case England had a role to play, and allies to play it with, and thus, despite her small land forces, she was able to matter in Europe. After the defeat of France in 1870, this position of diplomatic strength vanished. France entered into a long convalescence. The French army could no longer help contain Russia. The British navy was no longer needed by the imperial powers to contain French ambitions. Disraeli's Britain, unlike Palmerston's, was alone in Europe—alone in a world of giant conscript armies with only a small professional army and a rather irrelevant navy. It was not Disraeli's fault that he had so little leverage; rather, it was to his credit (or, as Salisbury thought, to Salisbury's) that he made such large paper gains at the Treaty of Berlin. But, like other Victorian Premiers, he was trapped within the pretence that one could have a foreign policy without having a defence policy; that one could be a great power on the cheap, and achieve large results with only the shadow of an army. Britain had effectively demobilized in 1815 because of the unwillingness of the gentry to pay taxes; Disraeli did nothing to reverse that fundamental decision.

Scholars are in general agreement about Disraeli's approach to practical politics. Studies of his part in the Second Reform Bill (by F. B. Smith and Maurice Cowling); of his social policy (by Paul Smith); of his protectionist period (by Robert Stewart); and of his life as a whole (by Lord Blake), all reach essentially the same conclusion—that as a practical politician he was largely uninfluenced by principles or beliefs. The most recent book (by Richard Millman, *Britain and the Eastern Crisis 1875–1878*) concludes that 'Disraeli, whose flexibility on policy was nearly total, was prepared for any Ottoman sacrifice consistent with British prestige'. Conservative political diaries, such as those of Derby, Carnarvon, and Gathorne Hardy, leave this existing interpretation unchanged, while revising our views of incidents, atmosphere, sub-plots, and personality. Thus we find Disraeli privately criticizing the Queen for being 'very wild', spoilt, and inconsiderate, while buttering her up as 'the Faery'; and it emerges that at the crucial Cabinet meeting at which the purchase of the Suez Canal shares was decided upon, Disraeli did not speak. He even fell asleep in Cabinet, for the first time, during the discussion of his celebrated trade-union legislation.

Our opinion of Disraeli is still based to a surprising degree on Disraeli's own reports of his triumphs. There is detective work to be done here—as there is also on the less respectable areas of intrigue that have so far been hidden from public gaze. But in the end he must be judged as a party man, as someone who failed to escape from the narrow dimensions of party to those of government, and whose greatest failure lay precisely in the area where he was most at home: party leadership. The more one sees Disraeli through the eyes of other Conservatives, the more one is aware of his failure to put down roots in his own party. Before 1868 he was tolerated because he was expected to retire with Derby; after 1868 he was tolerated, rather as Palmerston had been, because he was not expected to last long anyway. There was an attempt to remove him in 1872; and as early as 1874, his first year of office, he looked too ill to go on. Had Disraeli not appeared such a creaking gate, his colleagues would not have tolerated him so willingly. The period after the 1868 election defeat must be seen as the war of the Disraelian succession, a subdued race for a throne that might fall vacant at any time. From 1849 to 1881 Disraeli held his position only on sufferance; it was only posthumously that he became the inspiration of his party.

6 The Earlier Writings

DISRAELI'S novels have never lacked intelligent, if unlikely, admirers. The great Victorian critic Sir Leslie Stephen, inventor of muscular atheism, warmly approved. The equally austere Dr Leavis, in the least damnatory footnote in *The Great Tradition*, singled out Disraeli as a supreme intelligence. In youth, Disraeli was saluted by Heine; in age, Henry James wrote in his defence. The reviewer and Labour leader Michael Foot (who called his dog Dizzy) has argued brilliantly that Disraeli's novels were a magnificent denunciation of the cold, dull, purposeless, unimaginative Tory world. Only Trollope, a Liberal and a keen partisan of Thackeray (so maliciously attacked in *Endymion*), jealously denounced Disraeli's novels as flashy frippery.

Yet Disraeli wrote much trash, and much of his trash is bad trash: that is, it fails even to entertain or to give passing pleasure. His later works all succeed, or succeed in patches, but they are in the minority: *Coningsby* (1844), *Sybil* (1845), *Tancred* (1847), *Lord George Bentinck* (1852), *Lothair* (1870), and *Endymion* (1880), all written in the intervals of a busy political career. Even here there is much unevenness, a readiness to revert to type when pressed for time or when bored. The latter part of *Tancred* is inconsequential, religiose, and, as a story, absurd; the second part of *Lothair* is a ludicrous melodrama-cum-travelogue which fits ill with the acute social comedy of the first part. Disraeli never relinquished his gift for absurdity and bathos, for mixing incompatible genres within one cover. But it is the early works, now very much the preserve of Disraeli enthusiasts and hobbyists, which neither could nor should be revived. Their biographical, psychological, and political interest is considerable; as literature, they are slight.

Disraeli published sixteen titles before his Young England

phase: that is, his seventeenth book was his first good one. There were reasons for this, quite apart from youth, haste, and financial pressure. Two books were co-authored: *Gallomania* (1832) and *Hartlebury* (1834). Two were in verse: *The Revolutionary Epick* (1834) and *Count Alarcos* (1839), both bad of their kind. None, save *The Wondrous Tale of Alroy* (1833), had the Jewish motif that was to become so remarkable once Sidonia had made his first appearance in *Coningsby. Henrietta Temple* (1837) and *Venetia* (1837) were, as romantic novels, moderately good of their kind, but their pretensions were romantic, not intellectual or social. *Gallomania* (1832), the *Vindication* (1836), the *Letters of Runnymede* (1836), and the ephemera posthumously published as *Whigs and Whiggism* were political works, looking forward at times to the Young England Toryism of the next decade, but defaced by immediate polemical purpose, often of the crudest kind. Throughout these earlier writings religion is nowhere a preoccupation, and social questions are conspicuously absent. (A possible exception is the anti-utilitarianism of the skit *Popanilla* (1828) and of the semi-philosophic *Vindication*.) Sometimes, as with *The Young Duke* (1831), Disraeli's motive in writing was narrowly financial: literary prostitution, as he called it. Had Disraeli written none of these works, his reputation would stand higher today.

Vivian Grey (1826–7) is a young man's book. In its hopes, its gaucheries, its despairs, it is perhaps the youngest young man's book ever to attain wide fame. It is an account of society—high society and high politics—by an untutored middle-class town boy who had never experienced either. Despite that, it took society by storm; even after its early exposure, it attracted readers and was for a long time the book by which Disraeli was best known. Its very audacity breathes genius. From internal evidence, the great scholar Lucien Wolf suggests that its 80,000 words were written in about three weeks: an amazing feat. 'As hot and hurried a sketch as ever yet was penned', is how Disraeli describes it (*VG* i.236). Its story is as fascinated and half-horrified a self-exposure as any in romantic literature.

Vivian Grey, who outwardly resembles Disraeli at 21, finds out early that he is of no common clay. 'Mankind, then, is my great game.' (*VG* i. 26.) As his all-wise father, a tender portrait of Isaac D'Israeli, observes: 'Vivian, you are a juggler' (*VG* i. 182). Vivian's flair for manipulation encounters a corrupt adult world: he was 'a young and tender plant in a moral hot-house. His character was developing itself too soon.' (*VG* i. 24.) School barely over, he conquers society; but finding that he 'had all the desires of a matured mind—of an experienced man, but without maturity and experience', his thoughts turn to power. Encountering a *passé* statesman, the Marquess of Carabas, he persuades him and others in the great world that England sighs for a Carabas party—with Vivian Grey making the arrangements. With callous dexterity and supreme contempt for those he manipulates, Vivian Grey assembles a great national party, only to find it fall apart amid bitter recriminations. The story ought to end here, with Vivian Grey a ruined boy. It ought to, but unfortunately it does not. It continues for several hundred pages, with Vivian Grey, now penitent, wandering misanthropically round the Rhineland. This sequel is so entirely different in mood and style, not to say merit, that mankind has universally disregarded the second volume. It contains crumbs of evidence about Disraeli's state of mind; but it is not talented, and therefore it is not Disraelian.

Too much attention has always been focused on the circumstances surrounding the publication of *Vivian Grey*, and too little on its contents. The book, not the background, is the thing; and though he disavowed it as early as 1829 as a 'juvenile indiscretion', Disraeli's portrait of the superficiality of the high society he had never entered showed the power to create a coherent imaginary world. At 21, Disraeli had decided that the eminent and established were to be seen through. With few exceptions, he never changed his opinion.

But *Vivian Grey* was not a work of self-glorification. On the contrary, it was the record of the humbling of 'early vices and early follies'; it was, as Lucien Wolf writes, 'a retrospect, not an anticipation'. Grey is built up in order that he be knocked down. Above all, Disraeli is *not* Vivian Grey. As Wolf says: 'there is a narrator as well as a hero, and the philosophy of one is not the philosophy of the other' (*VG* i, p.xxxvii). 'Of the vices of Vivian Grey', writes Disraeli, 'no one is perhaps more sensible than their author.' (ibid.) The novelist of 1826 was looking back in remorse on the unlucky adventurer of 1825. That was the year in which Disraeli had tried to effect a great combination among his elders; but it was a middle-class affair, an attempt to induce the great publisher John Murray, who is Carabas, to set up a new daily paper. It is a long story, and still by no means a clear one; but nobody doubts that *Vivian Grey* is disguised autobiography, the record of hopeless, and probably final, failure. 'I have seen too much of politics', says Vivian Grey, 'ever to want to meddle with them again.' (*VG* ii. 89.) For the 'literary vices' of the novel, which indeed at points resembled Daisy Ashford's *The Young Visiters*, Disraeli apologized; but, he added, 'there is nothing written in it of which I am morally ashamed', meaning that it was a salutary tale—as indeed it is.

Two incidental points may be noticed. In Stapylton Toad, the forerunner of the immortal Tadpole in *Coningsby*, we see Disraeli's genius for creating minor characters. The unlovable Toad, moreover, anticipates Disraeli's own role in 1846 of being a hired gun in the defence of the Corn Laws: all in the way of business, of course. Also worth noting is the Tristram Shandyish chapter, 'The Development of the Plot' (*VG* i. 201–6), where Disraeli writes, and writes well, about the composition of *Vivian Grey*, mimicking in his sentences the actual discontinuities and interruptions in an author's thought. This reminds us that Disraeli, even in his first novel, was not just a fluent and intense writer, but also an experimental one, interested in redrawing the boundaries of literary genre.

Was *Vivian Grey* the production of a charlatan or of a boy? The question is idle. His portrait of political nature was right in its essentials, wrong in the inessentials. The charlatanism was only skin-deep. Vanity, egotism, the wish for attention; in all these, he demonstrated, the senate resembled the nursery. This great truth had not previously been set out with such uncompromising force in a political novel. *Vivian Grey* is no youthful error; it lays the ground for all that follows. And it is fun.

Popanilla (1828), a product of Disraeli's years of nervous breakdown, is a quaint, disrespectful, semi-radical, not very funny or biting satire on British society. For literary models, it used Voltaire's *Candide*, Johnson's *Rasselas*, and Thomas Love Peacock's recent novels of philosophic comedy: all hard acts to follow. The hero, Popanilla, a handsome youth, 'the delight of society and the especial favourite of the women', lived happily on a hedonistic tropical isle until stirred to rationality by the chance shipwreck of some utilitarian tracts. Roused to seriousness, he travelled to Vraibleusia (Britain), a country whose motto is 'something will turn up'. There he looks at national institutions (currency, law, trade, aristocracy) through utilitarian spectacles.

Utility itself is Disraeli's main object of ridicule, but there are others: in particular the Corn Laws. One conceit relates to a monopolist proprietor whose acres produced the only corn of the country, and who made the islanders purchase only from him: he 'swore it was the constitution of the country . . . He then clearly proved to them that, if ever they had the imprudence to change any of their old laws, they would necessarily never have more than one meal a day as long as they lived. Finally he recalled to their recollection that he made the island what it was . . .' (*P* 410–11). Such a mockery of the stock protectionist arguments made Disraeli the first literary Cobdenite—the more so as the anti-protectionism first hinted at in *Vivian Grey* was to appear in stronger form in *Coningsby* and *Sybil*. In another passage a 'total revolution was occasioned by the prohibition of foreign pineapples.

What an argument in favour of free trade!' (*P* 469.) *Popanilla* is too long for a skit, too lacking in direction for a satire. It is a readable, boyish experiment which offers only a few clues to the invention of the Tory Disraeli.

The Young Duke (1831) was a novel of fashionable life, written, with tongue in cheek, to provide funds for Disraeli's Mediterranean travels of 1830–1: 'I fear I must hack for it. A literary prostitute I have never yet been . . .'; 'I am confident that it will complete the corruption of the public taste.' Disraeli disliked it in retrospect, and regretted having written it. He drastically expurgated it in the 1853 edition of his works, and in his General Preface of 1870 he mentions it not at all. In this he was almost, but not quite, right. *The Young Duke* is a mechanical production, a typical 'silver fork' novel produced almost to a formula. As a whole, the best case that can be made for it is that it is enjoyable light reading.

This was inevitable. Disraeli at this time knew neither high society nor women; the novel was about little else, and Disraeli had nothing to say about either. 'What does Ben know about Dukes?', asked his father. It was a fair question to ask about an unemployed middle-class youth in his third year of nervous breakdown. But intelligence will out—even though writing with the express intention of not being himself, and of distancing himself and his hero from the creed of the amoral superboy celebrated in *Vivian Grey* (his subtitle is *A Moral Tale, though Gay*). Disraeli did not entirely confine himself to 'the fleeting manners of a somewhat frivolous age'. 'Let me die eating ortolans to the sound of soft music!' (*YD* 33.) This recalls Sydney Smith's undatable remark about heaven being eating pâté de foie gras to the sound of trumpets. Who, if anyone, plagiarized whom? We do not know. Radicals seized on this view of life, characteristic of much of *The Young Duke*, as sybaritic, 'très snob', and void of meaning. In fact, it was a search for meaning, for redemption by intensity; as Disraeli continues: 'At no time of his life had the Duke felt existence so intense.' From Disraeli's dandyism to the solemn aestheticism of Baudelaire and Pater is no long step.

Only in the final stages of *The Young Duke* does Disraeli turn to flexing his literary muscles. He gives us fleeting sketches of statesmen, including a disdainful one of Peel (*YD* 287). We see a prototype of George Eliot's Mrs Poyser (*YD* 270–2), a forerunner of Dickens's Mr Gradgrind (*YD* 289–97), and even a cockney soldier from India on the Kipling model (*YD* 293–6). As in *Popanilla*, the utilitarians are mocked, no doubt echoing Thomas Love Peacock, master of the genre; but it reminds us that Disraeli was anti-utilitarian long before he was a party Tory.

Disraeli's own Byronic unhappiness at this time breaks through in passages of unusual feeling:

For genius to be conscious that its supernatural energies might die away without creating their miracles: can the wheel or the rack rival the tortures of such a suspicion? . . . View the obscure Napoleon starving in the streets of Paris! What was St. Helena to the bitterness of such existence? (*YD* 82.)

Bitter are hope deferred, and self-reproach, and power unrecognised . . . But bitterer far than this, than these, than all, is waking from our first delusion! For then we first feel the nothingness of self: that hell of sanguine spirits. All is dreary, blank and cold. (*YD* 117–18.)

Disraeli, as *The Young Duke* shows, could have turned his pen to demotic social comedy, or analysed the nature of depression; but there was no demand for a Dickens, so he did the market's bidding.

Contarini Fleming, A Psychological Romance (1832) invites peremptory judgement. As psychology it lives; as romance it is insipid; as autobiography, tantalizing. Where childhood, youth, and family are concerned it is intense; where passion or the ways of man are involved it is a pot-boiler. Yet Heine, no mean critic, praised it warmly. Disraeli certainly intended it as a serious contribution to literature, and for that reason it is perhaps the best of his early works. Or would have been, had he not fallen foul of the grim requirement to fill three volumes, as publishers then demanded. Even Disraeli could not make examination of his own ego extend beyond two volumes, and so the novel collapses in the last hundred pages. It ceases to be a novel, and becomes a Mediterranean travelogue instead. ('The Spanish women are very interesting'.) Of Switzerland we learn, 'there is something magical in the mountain air' (*CF* 192–5); of a Turkish bath, that it is the most delightful thing in the world (*CF* 245). Commonplaces indeed! Albania, Athens, Jerusalem, Venice, Spain—Disraeli unblushingly retraced his recent tour, and locality did duty for character.

Disraeli's inimitable gift for bathos emerged in the ending. His hero, having seen and suffered all, retires to the Bay of Naples to build a 'Saracenic' palace for his art treasures, with a sphinx at each end of the terrace, and a tower 150 feet high. 'This tower I shall dedicate to the Future, and I intend that it shall be my tomb.' Disraeli was not good at endings. That apart, *Contarini Fleming* (first published anonymously) is about the development of the poetic character, the growth of identity in youth, the 'individual experience of self-formation'—a theme central to Disraeli's early work. By poetic character we should not understand just the character of a man who writes poetry: the poet is the man with an intellectual and political vocation. The discovery of vocation, often miscalled ambition, in youth is what still resounds in *Contarini Fleming*.

The novel takes place as much within the self as outside it, hence the necessity for an autobiographical form. 'In the earlier stages . . . the self-discoverer seemed an indispensable agent. What narrative by a third person could sufficiently paint the melancholy and brooding childhood, the first indications of the predisposition, the growing consciousness of power, the reveries, the loneliness, the doubts, the moody misery, the ignorance of art, the failures, the despair?' (*CF*, p. vi.) The story is simple. Young Contarini, son of a Swedish nobleman and Foreign Secretary, grows up in his northern land, uneasily aware that his true nature comes from his mother, the daughter of a great Venetian family, who died at his birth. He felt alien: 'I knew not why, but I was unhappy.' He felt remote from his stepmother and his two stepbrothers: 'There was no similitude between us.' Race played a part in this: the stepbrothers were 'my white brethren'.

As in *Venetia*, it is the mother–son relationship which queers the pitch, and from which all else arises. 'She was cold and I was repulsive.' (*CF* 6.) He develops 'a loathing for the government of women', and 'a contempt for the chatter of women' (*CF* 8, 16). Only when fleeing to his father's embrace did matters improve: 'For the first time in my life I felt happy, because, for the first time in my life, I felt loved.' (*CF* 7.) From disinheritance came depression:

I know not how it was, but the fit came upon me in an instant, and often when least counted on. A star, a sunset, a tree, a note of music, the sound of the wind, a fair face flitting by me in unknown beauty, and I was lost. All seemed vapid, dull, spiritless, and flat. Life had no object and no beauty; and I slunk to some solitary corner, where I was content to lie down and die. These were moments of agony . . . At last I had such a lengthened fit that it attracted universal attention. I would scarcely move, or speak, or eat for days. . . . Now that I can analyse my past feelings, these dark humours arose only from the want of being loved. (*CF* 18.)

At school he remained the outsider. For a time the passion of schoolboy friendship, described in a classic passage, absorbed his mind: 'I lavished upon him all the fanciful love that I had long stored up.' (*CF* 26.) Then his father 'talked to me for an unusual time upon the subject of school friendships, and his conversation, which was rare, made an impression' (*CF* 32). The objection was that Contarini's friend was a bumpkin. Contarini dropped his friend, provoking the anger of his school, and ran away, another episode paralleled in *Venetia*. Thus does Contarini explain himself at the end of his school life: 'But I have ever been unhappy, because I am perplexed about myself. I feel that I am not like other persons . . .' (*CF* 52).

From early deprivation grew his passion to excel, whether

in literature or in politics. At school 'I perceived only beings I was determined to control.' Later 'I entertained . . . a deep conviction that life must be intolerable unless I were the greatest of men.' (*CF* 29.) At 18 or so, told by his wise and loving father that 'with words we govern men', Contarini still harks back to early sorrows: 'I am always unhappy . . . There is no one who loves me . . . Life is intolerable to me, and I wish to die . . . What is the Baroness to me? Always this wretched nursery view of life, always considered an insignificant, unmeaning child!' (*CF* 102–3.) Thereafter Contarini's adventures lose inner content. He goes to university, wins a learned prize, discovers Voltaire, founds a Secret Union for the Amelioration of Society, and absconds to form a robber band. Then, despite 'my natural impatience of control and hatred of responsibility', he returns to act as private secretary to his father, to write a satirical novel (*Vivian Grey*), states that 'Fame, although not posthumous fame, is necessary to my felicity', and runs off, inconsequentially, to Venice, a tragic marriage, and some even more inconsequential Mediterranean travels.

Some Disraelian crumbs may be noted. 'There is no character in the world higher bred than a Turk of rank', he wrote (*CF* 320). He formulated a revolutionary system of poetics based on his objection to poetry being 'natural feelings in unnatural language' (*CF* 269–71). And he recalls that 'when a boy . . . I believed I had a predisposition for conspiracies' (*CF* 208). Three passages stand out as having a meaning that extends beyond the pages of the novel: 'Truly may I say that on the plains of Syria I parted for ever with my ambition. The calm enjoyment of existence appeared to me, as it now does, the highest attainable felicity . . .' (*CF* 343). Then come two political texts which could have fallen from the lips of a congenital radical: 'Bitter jest, that the most civilised portion of the globe should be considered incapable of self-government! When I examine the state of European society with the unimpassioned spirit which the philosopher can alone command, I perceive that it is in a state of transition from feudal to federal principles.' (*CF* 372.) Whatever that meant, it was not traditional Toryism.

Yet if I am to be remembered, let me be remembered as one who, in a sad night of gloomy ignorance and savage bigotry was prescient of the flaming morning-break of bright philosophy, as one who deeply sympathises with his fellow-men, and felt a proud and profound conviction of their perfectibility; as one who devoted himself to the amelioration of his kind, by the destruction of error and the propagation of truth. (*CF* 373.)

Behind the literary flourishes, Disraeli is saying that he is a reformer, a man of 1832; as indeed he was (and as Gladstone was not). Disraeli the Tory hero is hard to find in the self-absorbed romanticism of *Contarini Fleming*; while the Disraeli who, in his diary, claimed to have 'a revolutionary mind' is fitfully present, restrained only by an almost undue reverence for an idealized father.

But there is a twist in the tail. Consider the novel as a whole, especially the early parts. If politics start in the struggles of the nursery; if the nursery is the most intense part of life; if life is an aesthetic exercise in self-realization and self-creation; if all is subjectivity—then what becomes of the Enlightenment values of rational liberalism? *Contarini Fleming* was far ahead of its time not exactly in its politics, but in its portrayal of the way politics can grow out of a son's hatred for his mother. No other novelist before Lawrence attempted such a theme.

Most modern critics, writes Lord Blake, would attribute no merit whatever to *The Wondrous Tale of Alroy* (1833), 'which is written in a deplorable sort of prose-poetry and is perhaps the most unreadable of his romances' (B 108). Schwarz calls *Alroy* 'Disraeli's ultimate heroic fantasy' (Schw. 42); important for the author, though less so for his readers, because the book was not as unsuccessful as its predecessor *Contarini Fleming*, earning Disraeli £300 against *Fleming*'s £18. It proved, however, that Disraeli was never likely to be a popular success again so long as he said what he thought or wrote in the way he wanted. The public did not want Disraeli neat; *Alroy* was a landmark in the retreat towards the conventional story-telling of *Henrietta Temple* and *Venetia*.

At first sight, *Alroy* is poor man's Sir Walter Scott, with a touch of poor man's Byron. It is a historical novel, in full period costume. David Alroy, a medieval prince of the Jewish captivity, overthrows his Muslim masters and sets up a Jewish empire of Asia, based on Baghdad, before he is then overthrown. He dies a Jewish martyr, preferring death to apostasy. Its stage effects require no comment. There is much cleaving of skulls, flashing of scimitars, and use of magic talismans. The din of battles resounds. If tales of adventure are unreadable, then *Alroy* is unreadable. The psychology is equally predictable. Alroy is the standard Byronic hero, 'a mind to whose supreme volition the fortunes of the world would bow like fate' (*A* 187). Subjectively, he has a troubled mind: 'I know not what I feel, yet what I feel is madness.' (Schw. 43.) He cannot sleep, yet seeks 'glory, eternal glory', and finds the necessary therapy for his *mal du siècle* in action. 'Say what they like, man is made for action', is his doctrine (*A* 166)—and perhaps the author's too, for Disraeli later wrote that Alroy represented his 'ideal ambition'. The connection between mental disturbance, even weakness, and human greatness is just beneath the surface.

Alroy is important because of its Jewishness. Of Disraeli's first seventeen or so titles (those before *Coningsby*, with its Jewish sage Sidonia), it is the only one with significant Jewish content. To Disraeli its merit lay in its being 'the celebration of a gorgeous incident in the annals of that sacred and romantic people from whom I derive my blood'. He conveyed a true sense of Jewish lowliness: 'in Jerusalem, our people speak only in a whisper' (*A* 101). Do not blame Muslim oppression, he adds; Christian (or Jewish) intolerance, Disraeli makes clear, would have been worse: 'A Turk is a brute, but a Christian is a demon.' (*A* 101.) There was nothing anti-Muslim in Disraeli's revivalism.

Hope unfulfilled is at the heart of Disraeli's Judaism, as

it was also of his personal affairs when, as a young man at a loose end, he produced *Alroy*. When he wrote: 'if thou were greeted only with the cuff and the curse; if thou didst rise each morning only to feel existence to be dishonour, and to find thyself marked out among surrounding men as something foul and fatal; if it were thy lot . . . at best to drag on a mean and dull career, hopeless and aimless . . . and this all too with a keen sense of thy intrinsic worth, and a deep conviction of superior race' (*A* 78), Disraeli could be speaking either of his youthful débâcles or of the lot of the Jew everywhere. The two experiences, psychological and social, merge.

Disraeli's Jews are 'a proud and stiff-necked race, ever prone to rebellion' (*A* 130). They are warlike. They scoff at long rabbinical treatises. Disraeli's ideal of Jewish regeneration is decidedly military and is assisted by 'agents in every court, and camp, and cabinet' (*A* 157). (Would Disraeli have been so drawn to Jewishness had he not seen it as a vehicle for his beloved talent for conspiracy?) The drama of *Alroy* lies in the struggle of Jew against Jew. The victorious Alroy is a multiculturalist, as it were. He wishes to found a powerful Middle Eastern state in which Arab and Jew can live at ease with each other. To this end, he marries a Muslim princess, swears four Muslim nobles into his Council, and generally sets himself up as a liberal figure. 'Universal empire', he declares, 'must not be founded on sectarian prejudices and exclusive rights.' (*A* 187.)

Such rationalism, however magnanimous, hardly pleases the Jewish fundamentalists. Alroy wishes 'Baghdad to be my Sion'; he sneers at the thought of being 'the decent patriarch of a pastoral horde' (*A* 187) in impoverished Palestine. Theocracy in Israel, or empire in Baghdad; the rebuilding of the Temple, or military rejuvenation—these were not difficult alternatives on which to decide.

But Alroy fails, because he is no fanatic. He represents power unsupported by imagination. Against Alroy's imperial dream, his opponent the High Priest urges: 'You ask me what

I wish: my answer is, a national existence.' (*A* 204.) *Alroy* is Disraeli's anti-imperialist novel.

Which side was Disraeli on? It is hard to know, perhaps because he changed his mind half-way through. At first there seems no doubt. Alroy's secular realism is good; the High Priest's brooding intensity is sinister. Alroy is a boyish hero, a knight in shining armour. Yet by the end of the book the dying Alroy speaks in traditionalist, not latitudinarian, terms of Jewish destiny: 'My people stand apart from other nations, and ever will.' (*A* 329.) Here, surely, it is Alroy, the liberal figure, who has come round to the High Priest's unshakeable belief: 'We cannot mingle with them and yet be true to Him. We must exist alone. To preserve that loneliness, is the great end and essence of our law.' (*A* 207.) Besides struggle and spiritual purity, Disraeli offered, not without approval, a third form of Jewish redemption: upward social mobility based on uncompromising accommodation with existing power: 'Take my experience, child, and save yourself much sorrow . . . Freedom and honour are mine, but I was my own messiah.' (*A* 78–9.) So says the apostate court physician, confidant of the mighty, a calmly wise forerunner of Sidonia. Apostasy can be more than a Jewish vocation; it can itself be Messianic.

In *Alroy* Disraeli stated three predicaments: that of an oppressed race; that of a frustrated ambitious young man; and that of Jewish exclusiveness and the accommodation of Arabs (or indeed, political reality of any kind). All such questions are still with us. Disraeli had no solutions; but to find the West Bank in a light romance of 1833 is certainly curious.

Disraeli's prose poetry does not work, they say. Be that as it may, Disraeli wrote *Alroy* as a modernist in revolt against literary convention, and in the belief that he was a literary genius. His attempt to break the bounds of the customary language of fiction was ahead of its time. It would never do to forget that Disraeli was as ambitious in literature as he was in politics.

The Rise of Iskander (1833), a colourful adventure story, was published with *Alroy*, which it somewhat resembles. Both are romances of national liberation. *Alroy* concerns Jewish revolt against Islam; Iskander, or Scanderbeg, a medieval Albanian national hero, freed his people from the Turks. Though Iskander was mainly intent on abducting a Christian princess from the Turkish seraglio, there was at least a whiff of proto-Zionism to be found between the lines. Otherwise, guile and courage are the supreme human qualities, and none can withstand them: that is Disraeli's text.

Ixion in Heaven, a short magazine piece, is seen by admirers as a 'sparkling trifle'. Ixion, a peccant king on earth, is invited by Jove to Olympus, where the moral tone of the inhabitants curiously resembles that of London society. If it is a study in anything, it is in social climbing. Two gods talk thus of Ixion: ' "Not three days back an outcast among his own wretched species!" "and now commanding everybody in Heaven." ' Ixion does not lack confidence: 'These worthy Immortals required their minds to be opened, and I trust I have effectively performed the necessary operation ... To make your way in Heaven you must command. These exclusives sink under the audacious invention of an aspiring mind. ... I am a prime favourite.' Prime favourite indeed: Ixion ends up in the embrace of Juno. The cad will always win. *Ixion* is a metaphor for social ascent; its message, as in *Vivian Grey* or *Hartlebury*, is 'The Importance of Being Disraeli'.

The Infernal Marriage, published as a magazine piece in July–October 1834, is in the same vein as *Ixion*. As Lord Blake says, judged as 'light satires, modelled on Lucian, they have a freshness, wit and daring which still charm. Isaac [D'Israeli] considered them to be his son's most original contribution to literature.'(B 86). The apparatus is purely classical. Proserpine marries Pluto, King of Hades, hence the title; but we also pay visits to Olympus and Elysium. The gods, as in *Ixion*, have their origins in London society, but not so much so as to spoil the fable. The topical allusions, to Brougham and others, have faded; the classicism remains. (Apollo appears as the editor of a daily journal; Jupiter remarks: 'for my part I should only be too happy to extinguish the *Sun* and every other newspaper were it only in my power'.)

Slight though each is, *Iskander, Ixion,* and *The Infernal Marriage* can be used as evidence that Disraeli had the ease and inventiveness of the natural bellelettrist, the pure man of letters, writing from no intellectual or political motive, but seeking only to give passing amusement. Had circumstances required it, he could have carved a niche as a literary entertainer. A passage at the end of *The Infernal Marriage* gives some notion of how he saw felicity:

To wander in the green shade of secret woods and whisper our affection; to float on the sunny waters of some gentle stream, and listen to a serenade; to canter with a light-hearted cavalcade over breezy downs, or cool our panting chargers in the summer stillness of winding and woody lanes; to banquet with the beautiful and the witty; to send care to the devil, and indulge the whim of the moment; the priest, the warrior, and the statesman may frown and struggle as they like; but this is existence, and this, this is Elysium!

The sensuality of relaxation is more than a pose of Home Counties ruralism. It was so often stated, both publicly and privately, that it must have been an inner necessity. 'The green shade of woods' was a large part of the Disraelian ideology, and can be taken in two ways: either as contempt for public bustle, an assertion of the private; or as a characteristically conservative statement that politics are not the most important thing in life.

In 1979 the Canadian editors of Disraeli's letters discovered a long-forgotten novel, *Hartlebury, or The Election,* published pseudonymously in 1834. Most of it was written by Disraeli's sister Sarah; he contributed only an episode of fifty pages describing a borough election. Though Victorian novels are not short of election scenes set in country towns, *Hartlebury* is good of its kind: rattling, lively, and true to its period. Its main importance, however, lies in its portrayal of its brilliant hero, Mr Bohun, a thinly disguised version of Disraeli, and of his political ideas.

Mr Bohun, the local magnate, has (like Disraeli) just returned from the East. He combines a fine poetical temperament with a love of action. To women he was irresistible: 'God bless his curly locks', they cry. As an orator he combined 'inexhaustible sarcasm' with perorations of 'elaborate gorgeousness'. Bohun's motives owed more to Byron than to Burke. Politics was an extension of personality: 'This is life, this is excitement, and that is all I care about. I feel I live. For the rest, if I live I *must* be a great man.' This, surely, is Disraeli in the confessional.

Bohun's political method was modern. 'Agitate', he cried, 'agitate, agitate. That magic word is the essence of all political success.' All this, remember, was written half a decade before the Anti-Corn Law League. Because he was writing anonymously, Disraeli could be frank in presenting the Tory party as a vehicle for clever adventurers to ride mockingly for 'excitement'. Because gentry Toryism was moribund (or seemed so in 1834), its only chance lay in taking the side of 'the people' against the Whigs and their local oligarchy of sectarian high-street tradesmen. Though still only 'the Alcibiades of an obscure country town', Bohun wanted to see the formation of a new party, with himself at its head, on a truly national basis. Disraeli's answer to the débâcle of 1832 was to root Toryism as firmly in mass politics as Whiggism was among the shallower soil of the shopkeepers.

Hartlebury is Disraeli's *Mein Kampf*: it foreshadows, albeit patchily, much that lay ahead. The outmanoeuvring of the Whigs; a popular franchise; a social policy for the poor; the relation between individual genius and mass politics; and an anti-Whig sociology—all these can be traced there. It owes much to local events. Hartlebury is Bradenham, then the home of the Disraeli family, and the election takes place in neighbouring High Wycombe, which Disraeli had just lost, on a Radical–Tory platform, to the son of the Whig Prime Minister, Grey. From this trivial local episode, Disraeli proclaims the need to transform Toryism from an upper-class party of resistance to a broadly based popular party of national solidarity. The fictional message of *Hartlebury* coincides with the political theory of the *Vindication*: the Tories must become the party of the many.

The sole distinction of *The Revolutionary Epick* (1834), happily a work that was never completed, lay in its being the only epic ever written at Southend. Its lack of modesty was total. As Disraeli's original preface remarks, Greece, Rome, Florence, and Milton's England had all produced epics: 'And the spirit of my Time shall it alone be uncelebrated? ... Is Napoleon a less interesting character than Achilles? For me remains the Revolutionary Epick.' The first two books comprise the pleadings before a heavenly judge of two rival genii, one putting the case for the aristocratic principle, the other for the egalitarian or republican. Each scans history from antiquity to the present day. The third book, by an abrupt transition, jumps to Napoleon's Italian campaign; and there the project stops. The table of contents is promising at points (e.g. 'The State sacred: even its faults to be viewed with reverence'), but dissolves in a mechanical facility for versification.

Henrietta Temple: A Love Story (1836) and *Venetia* (1837) showed that Disraeli could produce readable middle-brow fiction more or less to order. It was fortunate that he could, for his finances were never more embarrassed than they were in these two years. Arrest for debt seemed imminent. A city deal had gone awry; and this was probably the reason for Disraeli's sudden need, in the latter part of 1836, to complete and publish *Henrietta Temple*, which he had begun three years earlier. The necessity to produce saleable fiction ended equally suddenly, a few months after the publication of *Venetia*, when in July 1837 he entered Parliament as MP for Maidstone. This gave him security from his creditors;

marriage to a fairly rich widow in 1839 enhanced his position, though his debts remained intermittently troublesome. Certainly, if it had not been for the electors of Maidstone, Disraeli would have had little choice but to continue his steady and mechanical production of what the literary market wanted. As it was, he published no prose in the years 1837 to 1844; between the ages of 32 and 39.

Henrietta Temple was a success, Disraeli's greatest hit with the public since *Vivian Grey*. It succeeded largely because it was so un-Disraelian. It contained no ideological baggage, no social message, no Jewishness, no religion, and no Toryism. Indeed, the hero was a Whig (though Disraeli by this time was an active Tory) who, though a member of the old Catholic gentry, never attends mass or makes confession, as one editor, Anthony Hern, points out. His Catholicism is an aesthetic stage prop, not a motif. 'We have no theatre for action', the hero complains, referring to the exclusion of Catholics from public life, but in fact he behaves like any other young man about town. Unlike Vivian Grey, Alroy, Ixion, Contarini Fleming, and Bohun, the young hero Ferdinand Armine is no Byronic genius born to conquer. Like Disraeli, he is an outsider (being Catholic), he is deeply indebted and in the clutches of the Jews (here unflatteringly portrayed), and he is a cad in need of redemption—in Armine's case, by love, entry into Parliament, and a lucky win of £15,000 at Crockford's by a generous friend. He has Disraeli's problems without Disraeli's talent.

Armine's difficulty, on which the story turns, is that he is engaged twice over: once to a rich cousin, heiress to the family estates, and a second time to Henrietta Temple, the love of his life. Henrietta finds out, retires to Italy, and seeks solace in an engagement to Lord Montfort. This obliging fellow, however, duly becomes attached to the rich cousin, leaving Ferdinand and Henrietta free to resume love at first sight. Of such stuff is romantic fiction made. But *Henrietta Temple: A Love Story* is not exactly what the title implies.

There is one obvious reason for this. Books 1–2 were written in 1833, when Disraeli was in love. They were then put in a drawer, and Books 3–6 were added, with 'a very terrible exertion', after Disraeli had put passion behind him. Thus, as with *Vivian Grey*, *Tancred*, and *Lothair*, an original impulse is resumed in a sequel that is written in a very different mood.

At first, love is all; but as the novel proceeds, love becomes one part, and a fairly subordinate part, of life's rich tapestry. We are after all in high society, where all agree 'that the man who permitted himself a moment's uneasiness about a woman was a fool' (*HT* 326). Disraeli presents such a view for our derision; but in the soberer part of the novel, he will only go so far as to offer this passionless dictum: 'A female friend, amicable, clever, and devoted, is a possession more valuable than parks and palaces; and without such a muse, few men can succeed in life, none be content.' (*HT* 160.) In fact, the novel is not story-telling pure and simple. It is about 'scrapes' (its key word): male scrapes. Of these the principal is passion, followed closely by debts. The answer to scrapes may in theory be the love of a good woman; but in practice, as *Henrietta Temple*'s later chapters show, the most effective remedy consists of a few choice male spirits sticking together. For a love story, there is a great deal of male bonding going on. We feel that the author, if asked to choose between perfect passion and having Count Mirabel as a chum, might be hard put to it. Mirabel, or D'Orsay, the great dandy to whom the book was dedicated, quite stole Henrietta's show.

Both as romance and West End social comedy, *Henrietta Temple* is a competent work by a practised hand. It is as free from intellectual ambition as a Trollope pot-boiler. But even so, there are two unremarked-upon passages where Disraeli's pen ran away with him. Both are declarations of a creed. Both are speeches of challenge and assertion. One, by Count Mirabel, the true hero of the novel and a partial forerunner of Sidonia, states his belief:

Existence is a pleasure, and the greatest. The world cannot rob us of that; and if it is better to live than to die, it is better to live in a good humour than a bad one. If a man be convinced that existence is the greatest pleasure, his happiness may be increased by good fortune, but it will be essentially independent of it. He who feels that the greatest source of pleasure always remains to him ought never to be miserable. (*HT* 328–9.)

Such was the philosophy of the adventurer; of the man, too, whom Disraeli always most admired as a great human being. A more Disraelian utterance comes in a set speech from a quite minor character, a former prize-fighter who has risen to vast, if dubious, wealth:

My position is difficult. I have risen by pursuits which the world does not consider reputable, yet if I had not recourse to them, I should be less than nothing. My mind, I think, is equal to my fortune: I am still young, and I would now avail myself of my power and establish myself in the land, a recognized member of society. But this cannot be. Society shrinks from an obscure foundling . . . Debarred therefore from a fair theatre for my energy and capital, I am forced to occupy, perhaps exhaust, myself in multiplied speculations . . . But I would gladly emancipate myself . . . Count Mirabel sympathizes with my situation. I believe he does not think, because a man has risen from an origin the most ignoble and obscure to a powerful position, by great courage and dexterity, and let me add also, by some profound thought, by struggling too, be it remembered, with a class of society as little scrupulous, though not so skilful as himself, that he is necessarily an infamous character. What if, at eighteen years of age, without a friend in the world . . . I flung myself into the ring? Who should be a gladiator if I were not? (*HT* 331–2.)

This apologia surely comes from the heart.

Was Disraeli feeling the strain of incipient respectability? *Venetia, or the Poet's Daughter* (1837), dedicated to the far from respectable Tory ex-Lord Chancellor Lord Lyndhurst, provided an answer of sorts. Lord Blake sees the novel as 'an awkward and artificial work, fatally marred by its whole concept—a fictionalized account of Byron and Shelley put back in the period of the American War of Independence' (B 146). As such, Blake, summarizing the views of Professor Jerman, calls it 'Disraeli's last tribute to the Byronic myth, a final protest against the respectable world'. There is much in this. Byron and Shelley were, in Tory eyes, men of the left. Moreover, their private lives were hardly conventional. To write about them was only to advertise to the world, and especially to the Tory world, all that was suspect about Disraeli. Where Armine had debts, Marmion Herbert (Shelley) had a mistress. Disraeli had had both; but why draw attention to the fact? Yet in his introduction Disraeli boldly commended Shelley and Byron as 'two of the most renowned and refined spirits that have adorned these, our latter days'.

While writing *Venetia*, Disraeli was in 'savagely gay' mood. He feared being 'nabbed' for debt, while hoping that William IV's failing health would shortly precipitate a general election. Disraeli had ideas of standing for Buckinghamshire, his home county and very much a gentry county; yet he intruded into *Venetia* a stock caricature of the rural magistrate, Squire Mountmeadow. On the face of it, prudence was not his dominant consideration. Yet, considering the possibilities of the subject (about which Disraeli had much inside knowledge), protest against convention is conspicuous by its absence. If in younger days Byron and Shelley set society by the ears, they were but the victims of misconception and priggishness. By the end of the story Shelley has settled down as a good family man: the perfect father and husband. We rub our eyes. Byron, too, though preaching the lower worldliness, does so while bathing in an innocent solitariness that is presented as his true self. The point being made here is not concerned with protest; it is that all scrapes pass in the end. As with *Henrietta Temple*, rehabilitation is the central preoccupation.

But again, have we not missed the central oddity of the novel? Namely, that this is a novel about Byron and Shelley in which Byron and Shelley play a surprisingly small part. To be exact, Shelley is firmly off-stage until page 212. He then, disconcertingly but without amplification, becomes a United States general on page 223; and finally emerges as a Venetian monk on page 381, ready to be a good father. This is all the stranger, as Disraeli chooses to make Shelley and his higher nonsense prevail over Byron's knowingness. Byron appears more as a schoolboy than anything else; it is not until page 229 that he emerges as a poet. To us today the two poets must be the focus of comment; but as the title states, this is a book about the poet's daughter, not the poet; about children and families, and especially about broken families. As Schwarz says, this is a novel about children; Disraeli's true preoccupation lay in being 'a psychologist of children, adolescents, and young adults, particularly members of those groups who are caught in emotionally claustrophobic circumstances' (Schw. 70).

In *Venetia* Disraeli was not doing himself any good politically. But he was not protesting either. He was celebrating the innate beauty of childhood and of the English countryside, and doing so with naturalness and authority. We cannot fit this into our picture of Disraeli the novelist of ideas, and we therefore push *Venetia* impatiently aside; but had it come from the pen of, say, Mark Rutherford or Trollope, it might be better regarded.

Count Alarcos (1839), a five-act blank-verse drama, is perhaps Disraeli's deadest work. Lord Blake calls it 'almost as destitute of literary merit as *The Revolutionary Epick*' (B 153). Intended as 'an attempt to contribute to the revival of English tragedy', it is an imitation of Shakespeare. If to write bad Shakespeare constitutes success, then it achieved success: the verse is springy, well-paced, and fluent. If nothing else, its archaic diction helps to link the modern romantic motive and the story set in a medieval Spanish court—Alarcos being 'the brightest knight, that ever waved a lance in Old Castille'. Alarcos had a problem; he had married the wrong woman, a woman he did not love. For Disraeli to take this as his theme in the year he made his own strange marriage was at least curious.

Very bad plays, and very bad verse, were normal in Victorian literature; Disraeli was far from being alone. It is puzzling, though, that he was pleased with his failure: 'Strange that I never wrote anything that was more talked of in society, and yet it has never been noticed by the scribbling critics,' Disraeli wrote. Nowhere is there the least trace of irony or thought, nor any hint that Disraeli was capable of a masterpiece in his next book. No route leads from *Count Alarcos* to *Coningsby*. Disraeli, at the ripe age of 35 and in the year of the Chartist Convention and revolt, had nothing to say.

7 The Young England Trilogy

THE Young England novels, *Coningsby* (1844), *Sybil* (1845), and *Tancred* (1847), form a trilogy distinct from Disraeli's other writings. Each asks a fundamental question. *Coningsby* asks: who rules? *Sybil* inquires: who ought to rule? *Tancred* debates: what to believe? Behind them lay a common theme: the condition of England. This was not a narrow matter of social problems in some limited sense—drains and trade unions, factories and the Poor Law. It concerned the more general issue of the terms on which power was to be held, and government by consent to be achieved. Disraeli raised that most continuous of Victorian preoccupations: how far did traditionalism in Church and State need to be modified to keep the show on the road? If he had a central purpose in the trilogy, it was to bring the gentlemen of England up to date. He wished them to see that by 'trusting the people' rather than opposing them, they might not only keep the show on the road, but actually strengthen their position. Seen in this perspective, the class conflict of the 1840s was a passing distemper, rich in opportunity. England's true nature lay in being a happy family under its natural leaders; but the question was, who were its natural leaders?

The problem of the poor was not primarily a problem of poverty. That was secondary to the question of who would use the poor as a power base: the social élite (the landed class) or the intellectual élite (the Chartists, the radicals, and their journalistic sympathizers). To some extent the answer lay in members of the social élite adopting an intellectual role and becoming men of ideas. Each novel in the trilogy features a young nobleman drawing away from his background in a quest for ideas capable of enabling him to lead his age.

One must ask oneself whether social compassion and anger are really present in the trilogy, or whether detached irony overlays them. The answer must be that detachment outweighs commitment, and irony all else. For all that, Disraeli had a strong sense of generosity as being something becoming in a gentleman—but as an incidental adornment, not a central purpose. He believed gentlemen should open their parks to the poor; he enjoyed the company of the Chiltern woodmen on his estate. But whereas Disraeli certainly went 'too far' where Jewishness was concerned, he was not stirred in the same way by poverty; there was a difference. (Indeed, at his Shrewsbury election in 1841 he had, thumb to nose, taunted proletarian hecklers as 'you young white factory niggers. [*Shower of missiles*] Oh, the very idea of seeing a gentleman frightens you.') What of Disraeli's solution? In modern terms, it would be that sociology is as much, or perhaps more, about values than it is about structures. Only *Sybil*, his Chartist or industrial novel, attempts to portray the structure of society as a whole, and does it very well. Never again did his pen venture more than fleetingly outside the world of society. Yet *Coningsby*, which is about the place of values in relation to political parties, and *Tancred*, with its search for a common ideology, were just as much 'solutions' to the problem of the age: how to unify modern urban society. Any solution, if such there were, clearly lay in the realm of belief, of a common culture; and such practical proposals as were abroad, like emigration, education, the factory movement, Corn Law repeal, church reform, and Poor Law reform, all fell short on this score.

Such proposals were too specific. They lacked a general idea. This Disraeli supplied: class peace, merging into mutual affection. This worked (albeit in very favourable economic circumstances). The Victorians adopted Disraeli's formula of class peace and class co-operation; after all, it cost nothing. Disraeli's failure to offer a panacea, in legislative terms, is often seen as a weak point, a sign of incompetent social engineering: should he not at least have urged a national almshouses service? In fact, his very generality was his strong point. His object was to find an attitude rather than a policy, and here the Young England approach was thoroughly modern. Because it was modern, it could not be Tory. Thus *Coningsby* (1844) depended upon a literary sleight of hand. While affecting to be anti-Whig, it was in reality venomously anti-Tory. By restricting true Toryism to a definition peculiar to the author, all actual Tories were placed firmly in the wrong. *Coningsby* may enrich the inheritance of every educated Englishman; it cannot gladden the Tory heart. In part, Disraeli's disgruntlement was personal. He owed the Tories nothing. He could, in 1844, see no future for himself in politics. A system that neglected his genius must have seemed one deserving of criticism. Moreover, he sat for Shrewsbury, a seat whose voters comprised all too many middle-class men who needed to be appeased. A novel by a Shrewsbury MP who wished to survive had to go easy on new men.

The tale echoes this. Young Coningsby, an Eton hero and one of nature's Tories, is heir to the great reactionary magnate Lord Monmouth, a monster of selfishness, who intends him to enter Parliament. Coningsby ends by telling Monmouth that he 'could not support the Conservative party' (*C* 359), and enters Parliament as an independent enjoying Liberal support, defeating the official Tory candidate. If the hero of a novel cannot support Conservatism, why should anyone else? It all depends, of course, what you mean by Conservatism. What Coningsby rejects is the purely negative Conservatism of Peel which 'would only embrace as much liberalism as is necessary for the moment; who wish to keep things as they find them for as long as they can' (*C* 309). Marching grudgingly from surrender to surrender; fighting a losing battle well; looking no further than getting the 'best bargain' from opponents who lay down the agenda: these Coningsby rejected. In modern terms, he (and Disraeli) wanted conviction politics to replace the ratchet effect of passive, ever-leftward movement. The Conservatives should set the agenda, but not in the wrong way; and much of *Coningsby* is a dazzling invective against the three wrong ways of being a Conservative.

In this *Coningsby* was modern, not archaic. It assumed that 1832 had changed everything. It saw a need to put the clock forward. It supposed that the gentry needed a new guide to survival. It praised Manchester, the middle class, manufacturers, and Lord John Russell. Only incidentally is it about political medievalism: maypoles, almsgiving, feast-days, and the need for property to acknowledge 'that labour is his twin brother' (*C* 362). Its central assumption was that Conservatism needed a new coat of paint. It derided three existing forms of Conservatism: administrative, manipulative, and reactionary. Lord Monmouth embodied suppression of the multitude; Tadpole and Taper, manipulation of the multitude; and Peel, administration of the multitude. Peel's offer of sound government—administration without imagination—was not enough. A modern statesman had to satisfy the imagination of the people. The reactionary Tory was equally a thing of the past, with his wish 'to put down the multitude' (*C* 62). Reaction was embodied in Lord Monmouth and in his factotum Rigby: 'There never was a fellow for giving a good hearty kick to the people like Rigby. Himself sprung from the dregs of the populace, this was disinterested.' (*C* 369.) Rigby, a portrait of a recognizable Tory publicist, was the villain of the novel. The manipulative Tory was seen in Tadpole and Taper, party wirepullers: 'Tadpole worshipped Registration; Taper advised a Cry. Tadpole always maintained that it was the winnowing of the electoral lists that could alone gain the day; Taper, on the contrary . . . was ever of opinion that the game must ultimately be won by popular clamour.' (*C* 409.)

As a novel of ideas, *Coningsby* is first and foremost an anti-Tory novel, cunningly disguised in the form of a search for the Holy Grail of a 'true Toryism'. It even derides Irish Protestantism (*C* 285, 357). As romantic fiction, it does not concern, though it may please, us. The apparatus is conventional. There is the mishap with a runaway horse (where would Victorian fiction be without equestrian accident?); the rumbustious election scene; the matrimonial intrigues; the stirring steeplechase; the unexpected codicil to a will—all these are the furniture of fiction. They do not stir the mind. To quarry *Coningsby* for its authorial message is the more legitimate since Disraeli's unit of thought was the rapid, scenic, self-contained chapter, and the author's pronouncements were concentrated in only a few of these. His non-fictional preoccupation was clear enough: what to do about the advent of mass politics? Resistance, even on the defences of the 1832 Act, was impossible. 'But who are the people? And where are you to draw the line? And why should there be any?' Exclusion was impossible. The £10 shopkeeper franchise of 1832 was an 'arbitrary, irrational, and impolitic qualification', leading inevitably to Chartism. The reformers had implicitly conceded the principle of universal suffrage (*C* 31–2). In writing a novel about the nature of political parties, Disraeli also posed the deeper question of what the old parties should do about mass politics.

Thus Book 1, otherwise a pretty tale of pretty Eton boys, emphasizes the contrast between youthful warmth and the hard-faced sterility of the pre-1832 hard right, represented by Lord Monmouth and Rigby. The hard right is not just unappealing; its real crime is that it is an anachronism and does not know it. Peel as an individual wins a wary respect; it was his elevation of pragmatism into an ideology in the *Tamworth Manifesto* (1834) that attracted Disraeli's derision.

Coningsby, unlike *Sybil* but like *Tancred*, has a Jewish motif, the first of Disraeli's works to do so since *Alroy*. Since Disraeli's philo-Semitism was racial rather than religious, *Coningsby* also contained a racial doctrine. In all this, the author's mouthpiece was Sidonia. Sidonia, the world's greatest capitalist, was not just Baron Rothschild in fictional dress. He represented other things too; the relation between intellectual and politician, for instance. He was not a victim of anti-Semitism, for 'though his religion walled him out from the pursuits of a citizen' (*C* 190), 'few men were more

85

popular, and none less understood' (*C* 194). Sidonia makes the point, not just a fictional one for Disraeli, that the English gentry and nobility among whom Disraeli had elected to spend his days were not a culture-bearing class. As Disraeli privately said: 'they never read, were out of touch with their times, and gave over their lives to field sports'. Hence the exaggeration of Sidonia's intellectuality by contrast.

Sidonia 'had exhausted all the sources of human knowledge; was master of the learning of every nation, of all tongues dead or living, of every literature, Western or Oriental. He had pursued the speculations of science . . . and had observed man under every phasis of civilisation.' He had that absolute 'freedom from prejudice, which was the compensatory possession of a man without a country' (*C* 189–90). At the centre of a network of 'secret agents and political spies', he held relations 'with all the clever outcasts of the world'. 'The secret history of the world was his pastime. His great pleasure was to contrast the hidden motive, with the public pretext, of transactions.' (*C* 191–2.) Sidonia was not Rothschild, except in terms of his fortune; was he then Disraeli? He bore no resemblance to anyone in the homely Jewish circles in which Disraeli had grown up. He was a mentor in search of a protégé; so, in 1844, was Disraeli. And he was as much psychologically as sociologically unusual. 'Woman was to him a toy, man a machine.' (*C* 190.) 'It was, of course, well known that Sidonia was not a marrying man.' (*C* 206.) Between Sidonia and Coningsby 'there at once occurred companionship . . . After a long ramble they would stretch themselves on the turf under a shady tree . . .' (*C* 206); 'no lady could accuse him of trifling with her feelings' (*C* 278). 'To find in another heart a perfect and profound sympathy . . . all this nature had denied to Sidonia.' (*C* 191.) 'The only human quality that interested Sidonia was Intellect.' (*C* 191.)

Sidonia embodies repression—but of what? It was because he 'shrank from sensibility' that the 'somewhat hard and literal character of English life so suited him' (*C* 193). The

Rothschilds, for all their ability, were family men. Sidonia was not; and his excuses—that he could not marry a Gentile, that he preferred *filles de joie*—only emerge by way of after-thought. Could it be, then, that Sidonia (or Disraeli) used a version of Jewish identity—the solitary bystander, the pure connoisseur of intellect—as sublimation for a psychological tendency? As a voice for Disraeli's views on race and Jewish-ness, Sidonia was a stroke of genius. His opinions were undoubtedly those of the author, and were thus considered in the chapters on race and religion. But his individuality was not necessarily intrinsically Jewish, and certainly was not the only form of Jewishness. It was more Byronism in Judaic garb, the cult of the man of genius. Sidonia was an external buttress to the main doctrine of *Coningsby*, that 'Brains every day become more precious than blood. You must give men new ideas, you must teach them new words, you must modify their manners, you must change their laws, you must root out prejudices, subvert convictions, if you wish to be great.' (*C* 401.) Sidonia, broadly considered, represented the claims of the intellectual in politics: the claim of intellect to equality with rank and fortune.

For a Young England novel, it is remarkable how little *Coningsby* contains of the the sentimental paternalism and medieval atavism that are usually seen as defining the move-ment; and how much any 'feudal socialism' is kept a thing apart from the main argument, entering the story as colour-ful depiction rather than recommendation. The embodiment of medievalism is Eustace Lyle, a young Catholic landowner (drawn from life) who runs a private welfare state with all due ceremony. He is a very minor character, appears only in two chapters, was not one of Coningsby's set at Eton out of which Young England grew, and has renounced any part in public life. In fact, Eustace Lyle is anything but a plea for state Welfarism. If he ceremoniously gave all his workers a basketful of beef, bread, and ale at Christmas, it was because he 'wished the people constantly and visibly to comprehend that Property is their protector and their friend'

(*C* 127). Lyle's festivities were 'a fresh argument' against 'a mere mechanical mitigation of the material necessities of the lower classes', a mitigation 'which must inevitably be limited'. Their condition, observes the author, was 'not merely a "knife-and-fork" question . . . a simple satisfaction of the grosser necessities of our nature will not make a happy people . . . you must cultivate the heart as well as seek to content the belly . . . the surest means to elevate the character of the people is to appeal to their affections' (*C* 388). Free food is not an end in itself, but a means to an end: social cohesion.

There are other, lesser, but more normal symbols of community: one rural, at Beaumanoir (Belvoir Castle, home of the Dukes of Rutland); the other the factory village owned by Millbank, with its library, lecture room, singing class, allotments, 'houses and cottages on a new system of ventilation'(*C* 141–3). No dark satanic mills here (or anywhere else in *Coningsby*). As at Beaumanoir, social well-being is a matter for the private sector. Nowhere is there any hint of collectivism or any call for the massive injection of state funds. *Coningsby,* by implication and omission, firmly excludes state social reform from the agenda.

In its references to Manchester, 'the most wonderful city of modern times', as Coningsby calls it (*C* 138), we see Disraeli's capitalist modernism at its most exuberant. 'Rightly understood, Manchester is as great an exploit as Athens', the author comments; because 'What Art was to the ancient world, Science is to the modern: the distinctive faculty.' 'It is the philosopher alone who can conceive the grandeur of Manchester, and the immensity of its future.' (*C* 134.) Sidonia agrees: 'The Age of Ruins is past. Have you seen Manchester?', he urges Coningsby (*C* 101), who thoughtfully ponders on how its wealth was 'rapidly developing classes whose power was imperfectly recognised in the constitutional scheme' (*C* 137). Politically as well as economically, standing still was not an option; Manchester symbolizes this. (Manchester as a symbol of proletarian misery—Disraeli was writing in the same year as Engels—is conspicuously absent.) As with Manchester, so with Millbank, the Liberal manufacturer and self-styled 'disciple of progress', whose rugged principle stood in stark contrast to the low cunning of the Tory fixer Rigby, a professional opponent of 'Liberal principles' by trade. Disraeli's escape from the middle class had left him with no wish ever to return to it; but publicly and as a matter of doctrine he had no quarrel with business, and was willing to make the sacrifice of treating it with respect.

Disraeli's attitude to commercial restrictions also makes it clear that *Coningsby* was not in revolt against, but an endorsement of, the modern market economy. Indeed, as an example of the advantage of free trade, he suggests lightly that if the French bought our pottery in exchange for their wines, they would for the first time 'dine off hot plates. An unanswerable instance of the advantages of commercial reciprocity!' (*C* 273.) More seriously, in the context of the 1841 election, he derides the squires and farmers whose 'Conservative principles' mean nothing higher 'than a perpetuation of fiscal arrangements, some of them impolitic, none of them important' (*C* 410). Such anti-Corn Law expressions were no accident, but the result of steady conviction, long expressed in Disraeli's earlier works and developed in the main historical survey in *Coningsby* (*C* 56–72). Here Disraeli damned the 'pseudo-Tories' who 'made Exclusion the principle of their political constitution, and Restriction the genius of their commercial code' (*C* 60). 'Exclusive principles in the constitution, and restrictive principles in commerce, have grown up together; and have really nothing in common with the ancient character of our political settlement . . .'. The 'three great elements . . . of the real Pitt system' were 'a widening of our electoral scheme, great facilities to commerce, and the rescue of our Roman Catholic fellow-subjects from the Puritanic yoke' (*C* 66). This came close to saying that the only true Toryism was to be found in modern liberalism. Certainly, in matters of trade Disraeli was an instinctive Peelite who associated fetters on commerce with the bad old days.

Disraeli may have had his reasons for writing as he did. He sat (insecurely) at this time for Shrewsbury, and may have been trying to square the circle in terms of constituency politics. Why, for instance, did he so inordinately praise the Liberal leader Lord John Russell as alone 'having that degree of imagination' which enables him to 'generalise from the details of his reading and experience' (*C* 245–6)? When Disraeli lavished similar praised on Palmerston, also ostensibly his political opponent, in *Tancred*, he was covertly acting as Palmerston's agent; so anything is possible.

At the core of *Coningsby* is a doctrine that political culture matters. Political culture is a question of platitudes, but they must be the right platitudes; and uttering the right platitudes requires genius. 'A great man is one who affects the mind of his generation.' 'The Spirit of the Age is the very thing that a great man changes.' (*C* 108, 104.) What public men say, not what they do, is the key to Disraeli's only real social policy: the achievement of an era of good feeling. It is in this sense that Disraeli is a 'social' thinker. When Sidonia says: 'I do not ascribe to political institutions that paramount influence which it is the feeling of the age to ascribe to them' (*C* 208), it is not social reform he is calling for, but social unity based on a sense of community. 'England should think more of the community and less of the government.' Disraeli's social doctrine is anti-statist. 'The peril of England' lies not in its institutions, but 'in the decline of its character as a community' (*C* 208). To twentieth-century collectivists, social unity and the big state have often seemed to be twin doctrines. Disraeli would not have agreed.

Disraeli assumed that aristocracy could not survive merely on its governmental merits. It needed slogans. 'If Democracy be combated only by Conservatism, Democracy must triumph . . .' (*C* 310). Mass politics could not be avoided. The Reform Bill itself might not have shaken aristocratic power; it was the means by which it was carried—the social power of new classes—that was the truly ugly portent (*C* 196). The post-1832 world was irredeemably modern. As Sidonia said: 'Society in this country is perplexed, almost paralysed . . . How are the elements of the nation to be again blended together? In what spirit is that reorganisation to take place?' (*C* 210.) Sidonia, let it be noted, the true voice of Disraelian prophecy, never proposed a return to feudal principles as a remedy. He foresaw the great danger of mass politics: that if men cease to believe in a fixed order of things, they will not believe in nothing; they will believe in anything. 'Man is made to adore and to obey; but if you will not command him, if you give him nothing to worship, he will fashion his own divinities, and find a chieftain in his own passions.' (*C* 209–10.) In a post-aristocratic world, only the recycling of aristocratic values in a classless or 'national' way can enable 'imagination' (or literary creativity) to save the state from the demons of mass politics.

Disraeli's remedies were less class conflict, a strong executive, and a government that was responsive to public opinion. That may not sound exciting, but platitudes are not meant to excite. Moreover, his propositions were not merely a shopping-list, but followed closely one from the other. If 'the decline of public virtue' arose from 'the fact that the various classes of this country are arrayed against each other', then 'the only way to terminate . . . class legislation is not to entrust power to classes. . . . The only power that has no class sympathy is the Sovereign.' (*C* 311.) A 'neglected democracy . . . who have received no education' (*C* 310), offered no hope; the liberal solution could be ruled out as a blind alley. Nor was an idolatrous regard for Parliament more abreast of the times. 'Parliamentary representation was the happy device of a ruder age', observes Coningsby; but the future lay with the media. 'An educated nation recoils from the imperfect vicariate of what is called a representative government', says Sidonia, hoping instead for 'public opinion' acting through 'one who has no class interests' (Mr Gladstone perhaps?).

91

Disraeli has been much laughed at as the man who wished to hand power back to the Hanoverians. Yet when he writes of 'the Sovereign', does he really mean Queen Victoria personally? One would hardly think so. Victoria was a Whig Queen, and not a popular one; an unsavoury court scandal that reflected directly on her was alluded to in *Coningsby*. In 1844 Disraeli had no motive for monarchism in any literal sense; but, as the opponent of 'the high aristocratic republic' and 'Venetian constitution [that] did govern England from the accession of the House of Hanover until 1832', he needed a term for something that was not Whig oligarchy. Perhaps his view was not far from Peel's own deeply felt doctrine of the rights and duties of Ministers of the Crown. At any rate, 'monarchy' in the sense of presidential rule is what has happened—always in England, and eventually elsewhere. The world is more presidential than parliamentary. We do not have Bagehot's 'government by discussion'. Disraeli foresaw that the divinity of Parliament would go the way of the divine right of kings.

Coningsby's quest began with his asking 'why governments were hated, and religion despised? Why loyalty was dead, and reverence only a galvanised corpse?' (*C* 109.) His eventual answer was 'the idea of a free monarchy, established on fundamental laws, itself the apex of a vast pile of municipal and local government, ruling an educated people, represented by a free and intellectual press . . . Now there is a polity . . . which . . . would render government an object of national affection . . . and extinguish Chartism.' (*C* 313.) Disraeli's criterion of good government, let it be said, was the affection in which it was held. In this he foreshadows that greatest healer among British Prime Ministers, Stanley Baldwin.

Sybil, or The Two Nations (1845) was Disraeli's social novel. It introduces us to the poor, both urban and rural. We see their poverty, their animality, and their political aspirations. From Blue Books came the pictures of misery; from contacts with radical politicians, the scenes of agitation. Such is the conventional view, and it is true as far as it goes. But *Sybil* is no mere documentary. It is a tract aimed at the aristocracy. If *Coningsby* asked: who rules?, *Sybil* asked: who ought to rule? The poor were a power base in search of direction. They might turn to intellectual leaders, such as Chartist radicals; they might look to their social leaders, the landowning class. Disraeli's aim was not only, or not mainly, to relieve misery, but to point to the opportunities awaiting a redeemed aristocracy.

The aristocracy as it was, against the aristocracy as it ought to be, was Disraeli's theme, just as much as the conflict of rich and poor. At the start of the book we encounter bored young aristocrats who had 'exhausted life in their teens'. Their life was dinners, horses, and Wildian wit: 'I rather like bad wine, one gets so bored with good wine.' They were an aristocracy for whom art, science, music did not exist. They were a functionless class, doing themselves out of a job.

Also doing his class out of a job, but in a far more aggressive way, was the magnate Lord Marney, busily grinding the face of the Yorkshire poor on his estates. Marney, 'arrogant, literal, hard . . . acute, disputatious, and firm even to obstinacy', was all that an aristocrat should not be. His principles of 'high prices and low church' could not be excused by rusticity, for, ominously, he had formed his mind on the materialist liberal thinker Helvétius. Worse, perhaps, was the fact that the Marney pedigree would not stand examination. Like the history of England itself, it was a sham, a mystification. The *arriviste* Marneys were the types of a parvenu aristocracy. A lowly Tudor clerk, one Greymount, had profited from the spoliation of monastic lands. By 1600 the plebeian Greymounts had become the 'Norman' Egremonts, Barons Marney: Cavalier in 1640, Whig in 1688, earls under William III. Earls, but not Dukes: for the other oligarchs did not support them. They had done 'none of the work of the last hundred years of political mystification, during which a people without power or education had been induced to believe themselves the freest and most enlightened nation in the world'. Unable to secure preferment from the old Whigs, the Marneys had to turn to Pitt, only to find that he diluted the peerage wholesale.

Pitt 'created a plebeian aristocracy and blended it with the patrician oligarchy. He made peers of second-rate squires and fat graziers. He caught them in the alleys of Lombard Street, and clutched them from the counting-houses of Cornhill.' Disraeli's point could not be clearer: there was nothing inherently aristocratic about the British aristocracy, no qualities of blood that might excuse their defects. The message recurs; the Fitz-Warens, Earls de Mowbray, neighbours of Marney, could not trace their descent any further back than one Warren, a sharp-witted club waiter who rose under George IV. Aristocracy, therefore, is neither pedigree nor blood; it is a set of rules to be learned—it is the art of governing by consent, of uniting all hearts. It is a skill, not a social position. Egremont, Lord Marney's younger brother, embodies the learning process.

Egremont, like Lothair and Endymion, is a vacuous anti-hero, a *naïf*, almost a prig, who drifts through his twenties, at a loss in a world where 'to do nothing and get something formed a boy's ideal of a manly career' (*S* 29). After Eton, Oxford, society, and travel, at 30 'he in fact knew nothing', least of all about his country and his place in it. The education of Egremont begins with his encounter with Sybil, her father Walter Gerard, and their companion Stephen Morley, a Chartist journalist. The meeting takes place among the ruins of Marney Abbey (based on Fountains), whose monks once typified true aristocracy. As ever, Disraeli's sympathy for Catholicism is aesthetic and social; never religious. In a brilliant dialogue of ideas, Egremont learns that there are two nations: 'THE RICH AND THE POOR' (*S* 65–6). The scene ends with a romantic sunset and the elder stranger playing to the sound of a beautiful girl's hymn: well enough, but a timeless moment is no remedy for social ills.

The use of the medieval abbey to symbolize an organic society that does not rest on the cash nexus paralleled Carlyle's *Past and Present* (1843). With all the pomp of modern sociology, the Chartist thinker mused on the distinction between *Gemeinschaft* and *Gesellschaft*:

As to community . . . with the monasteries expired the only type that we ever had in England of such an intercourse. There is no community in England: there is aggregation, but aggregation under circumstances which make it rather a dissociating, than a uniting, principle . . . I prefer association to gregariousness . . . It is a community of purpose that constitutes society, without that, men may be drawn into contiguity, but they still continue virtually isolated. . . . Modern society acknowledges no neighbour. (*S* 64–5.)

Familiar stuff, perhaps, today: not familiar in 1845. At first sight, Disraeli was preaching high-mindedly on the superiority of co-operation over individualism. His text, however, hardly supported this, for the two communities in *Sybil* were far from ideal. Wodgate, a Black Country manufacturing town without a gentleman or a church in it, showed a proletarian community in the grip of a proletarian aristocracy—and very nasty they were. The other community was a model mill-village: virtuous, but a prison, and lacking the fun and spirit Disraeli imputed to youth culture in the inner cities, with its self-seeking individualism.

The novel goes its own way, as novels do. Stephen Morley, the portentous social thinker encountered in the abbey ruins, becomes by degrees a thoroughly bad hat. Devilsdust, the inner-city trouble-maker, becomes an innovative capitalist. The reconciliation of rich and poor is achieved when Egremont marries Sybil, whose blue blood has been dramatically revealed; a reconciliation of rich and rich. Flexible though Disraeli was, he could not contemplate marriage outside one's class. The scenes from working-class life were just that: scenes. They were not a plea for a welfare state, a premonition of twentieth-century collectivism, or a sketch of an anti-liberal economic policy. Indeed, in *Sybil* Disraeli found room to pay tribute to the free-trade tradition which a year later he was to oppose so eloquently in Parliament. But they were very good scenes. Considering his ignorance, Disraeli showed remarkable range. There was Wodgate, the small industrial town. There was the commercial metropolis (Leeds?) where Devilsdust makes merry. There was the decayed rural slum of Marney (Ripon), proof that the absence of industrialism is not the answer. There was the radical underworld of London. If these vignettes had a moral, it was that the best place to be poor was a provincial metropolis like Leeds.

Was Disraeli's picture of the condition of England distorted? In some ways, yes. *Sybil* (1845) reflected the severe slump of 1842, not the prosperity and great railway boom of three years later. Moreover, as prosperity returned, corn prices fell; they were significantly lower in 1843–5 than they had been in 1837–42. Even in its first year of publication, *Sybil* was a historical novel. Disraeli tampered with the evidence in other ways. He made Wodgate churchless, when the original report showed otherwise; and with the Victorian reader in mind, he obliterated its health problems, such as the rotting heaps of human manure by each house. Faced with a choice between literary propriety and the chance to expose the drainage problem, Disraeli cautiously chose propriety.

Did *Sybil* advocate a social policy? Disraeli might say that 'the *social* happiness of the millions should be the first object of a statesman', before going on to blame 'cheap and centralised government'. In conventional progressive terms he backed none of the usual remedies: education, emigration, radical reform in Church and State. His broader formula of class peace, gentry rule, and letting the specific remedies drift was an attitude, not a programme. That it contained no panacea was its strongest point.

'Tancred is the Marquess of Montacute, adored only son of the virtuous but limited Duke and Duchess of Bellamont, and the book opens with his coming of age. To the consternation of his parents, he declines to enter parliament and declares his desire to visit the Holy Land in the hope that somehow he will receive an answer to the questions that have been silently troubling him.' (B 201.) Such, in outline, is the theme of *Tancred, or the New Crusade* (1847).

Tancred does indeed reach Jerusalem, where the lovely Eva engages him in Jewish–Christian dialogue; he visits Sinai and hears the Angel of Arabia; he is held to ransom by desert tribes; he emerges, the guest of the feudal Emir Fakredeen, in Lebanon; he meets a Syrian tribe who worship the gods of pagan antiquity; and he leads a desert uprising to found a pan-Arab empire, until put down by the Turks. Tancred hovers uncertainly between founding a great Asian empire, seeking religious truth, and wooing Eva; and it is as he awaits Eva's answer to his proposal that he learns his parents have arrived in Jerusalem. No more inconclusive conclusion could be imagined, unless a sequel were perhaps intended, with Eva as a Jewish duchess. The novel is a curious mixture of *Coningsby* and *Alroy:* more bitter that *Coningsby* where it deals with English society; as exotically personal as *Alroy* where the East is concerned. Mellowed by Disraeli's great success in 1846 it certainly was not, for the newly prominent author must have learned as never before what was said about him behind his back.

Tancred was Disraeli's favourite among his novels. Few have agreed with his choice. It is two-thirds an Eastern romance, one-third English social comedy: the two parts sit oddly together. The signs of social conscience that were displayed in *Sybil* are absent here. It is not political in the obvious sense, as *Coningsby* had been. It is not even ecclesiastical. Only three clerics appear. They march on, are made fun of, and are briskly marched off. The Church of England remains firmly outside the picture, an object of contempt. *Tancred* is in fact about race and about social cohesion, and the relation of both to belief. When Tancred, a young English noble, justifies his journey to Jerusalem by asking: 'What is DUTY, and what is FAITH? What ought I to DO, and what ought I to BELIEVE?', his quest is for a public doctrine which will bind society together, not for some form of churchiness. The idea that *Tancred* was Disraeli's 'church' novel will not do. It derives from Disraeli's various prefaces, including the General Preface of 1870, written when he had been heavily involved in church politics for a decade. Put these subsequent prefaces aside, and a different preoccupation emerges from the text.

The masses need an ideology, Disraeli says. How else can millions of urban beings, unknown to each other, live together? 'Europe is in the throes of a great birth ... The multitudes are again brooding ... they are in the cities and the fertile plains.' (*T* 290.) Revolution, the Revolution of 1848, is in the air in this novel written in 1845–6. 'Europe is not happy. Amid its false excitement, its bustling inventions, and its endless toil, a profound melancholy broods over its spirit and gnaws at its heart. In vain they baptize their tumult by the name of progress: the whisper of a demon is ever asking them "Progress, from whence and to what?" ' (*T* 309.)

'Announce the sublime and solacing doctrine of theocratic equality', the Angel of Arabia tells Tancred in a 'mystic' passage that is usually held to reek of charlatanism (*T* 291). But despite the religiosity of tone, the meaning is earthly: 'theocratic equality', or a moral order, is offered as 'the solution to the social problem that perplexes you' (*T* 291). This 'equality, properly developed, is in fact the patriarchal principle' (*T* 367), for 'the longing for fraternity can never be satisfied but under the sway of a common Father' (*T* 291): no Fatherhood, no brotherhood. Disraeli respects Islam for its sense of fraternity. He respects the revolutionaries for their pain at the lack of it. He does not respect liberal materialism, which fails to see that there is even a problem about how to create social cohesion and national identity: 'a society that has mistaken comfort for civilisation', he calls Europe (*T* 227).

In all this there is nothing specifically Christian, still less Judaic. Behind its showiness, Disraeli's message is that religion or ideology is socially necessary, or a means of social control. Such a view is one that can be strongly held by a man who was not a conventional believer, as Disraeli probably was not. *Tancred* is essentially a sincere statement of Disraeli's view that society without ideology, like government without imagination, is dangerous where it is not impossible. As the Angel of Arabia says: 'power is neither the sword nor the shield, for these pass away, but ideas, which are divine' (*T* 290). It is the role of ideas in general, not any single idea, that concerns Disraeli; and those who blame him for not offering a religious panacea miss the point.

Disraeli was looking forwards, not backwards, to a modern, post-feudal world where 'the principle of association [replaced] that of dependence as the foundation of the Commonwealth' (*T* 369). What modern mass ideology was needed to make 'association' work? Not a mere opposition mentality, which Disraeli condemned: 'the intellectual colony of Arabia, once called Christendom, has been in a state of partial and blind revolt' (*T* 290). Nor can the religious superstructure defy its material base: 'Europe is too proud, with its new command over nature, to listen even to prophets . . . How can these men believe that there is any power, human or divine, superior to themselves?' (*T* 309.) It is because the Supreme Being has never revealed his will to a European—as Tancred comes to think: 'there is a qualification of blood as well as of locality necessary for this communion' (*T* 262)—that an Asian novel is justified on more than scenic grounds. 'I must return to the Desert to recover the purity of my mind. It is Arabia alone that can regenerate the world', says Tancred (*T* 465). Revelation needed updating if Tancred's 'passive faith' in Anglicanism were to be turned into an 'active' faith fit for modernity. Disraeli's 'church' novel rejects, rather than embraces, traditional religion; in particular, it rejects all forms of contemporary Anglicanism.

Arabs, said Disraeli, are simply Jews on horseback, and very thoroughly does he apply this principle of Semitic unity. Christ is a 'Galilean Arab' (*T* 290). Tancred, riding in the Sinai Desert, is captured by a Bedouin sheikh. Surprisingly, the sheikh and his whole tribe are Jews, 'live in tents, have thousands of camels . . . and care for nothing except Jehovah, Moses, and their mares' (*T* 192). Disraeli is never anti-Islamic; Muhammad is treated more sympathetically than that ecclesiastical Peel, the Bishop of London.

If Jews were 'an Arabian tribe' (*T* 228), then both Arabs and Jews were superior versions of Europeans: Moses, for instance, was 'a man of the complete Caucasian model' (*T* 228). They inhabited a vast common homeland, Syria, which in Disraeli's eyes was not the modern state of that name, but stretched from Gaza to Aleppo, and from Gaza to the Euphrates (*T* 286, 344). There could be no Palestine problem, for Palestine, to Disraeli, was a Syrian province; and the liberation of Syria from the Turks (as nearly occurred in 1839) would, Disraeli hints heavily, as if from private knowledge, have given the signal for Jewish colonization. *Tancred* is an anti-Turkish book; Disraeli wanted an Arab Middle East for Jewish reasons. Had Tancred's empire succeeded, it would have been an Arab empire. 'A man might climb Mount Carmel', declares Tancred, 'and utter three words which would bring the Arabs again to Granada, and perhaps further.'

Disraeli clearly thought the oriental section of *Tancred* was important. Critics who dismiss it, as if criticism stopped at Calais, do not enter the author's mind. By overthrowing Peel, Disraeli had earned the right to speak out; and that indeed he did, regardless of reputation. No merely prudent man would have written *Tancred*; nor need he have done so on literary grounds, for his social comedy was as inventive as ever—who else at that time would have opened a novel with a scene set among the tribe of West End chefs? No: if Disraeli wrote 320 vivid, self-absorbed pages about the East, it was because he wished to feel that 'Europe is to Asia what

America is to Europe' (*T* 193). 'Christendom', wrote Disraeli, 'calls itself enlightened Europe. But enlightened Europe is not happy. Its existence is a fever, which it calls progress. Progress to what?' For Disraeli, to be anti-European and anti-Liberal were much the same thing; and he was fairly sincere in both attitudes. No man writes two books about Jewish revivalism and Eastern empires, as Disraeli did in *Alroy* and *Tancred*, unless the subject means something to him.

The idea of Arabia, or 'the great Asian mystery', is less important for what it espouses than for what it rejects: the secular idolatries of modern liberal Britain. The orientalism of *Tancred* is not just a literary device; far from it. The magical beauty of Jerusalem; the stony Arabian desert; the intricacies of Lebanese intrigue—these are all realities. This scenic basis apart, Disraeli, as Lord Blake disapprovingly says, appears 'to be arguing against the parliamentary system, against self-government, against "progress", against "reason"; and he apparently substitutes for them a sort of benevolent clerical monarchism supported by a conscientious aristocracy' (B 209). To Blake, this is 'unmistakably illiberal'; and Tancred does indeed talk wildly of 'crushing the political atheism that is now desolating existence', and 'utterly extinguishing the grovelling tyranny of self-government' (*T* 421).

In fact, to think sociologically, Disraeli was on the right lines. Late Victorian England, for all its nominal parliamentarianism, was largely governed by a strong executive drawn from a conscientious aristocracy, responsive, as all states always have been, to opinion; working with, rather than against, its 'clerisy' of clergy and intellectuals, and using monarchy as its symbol of unity. To say this in 1847, a time of troubles, was at worst to be ahead of time, at best to anticipate Bagehot's doctrine of the 'elegant façade' of English institutions which so disguised social (and class) realities. Disraeli, long a practised social ironist, was well fitted to expose secular pointlessness, Anglocentric parochiality, and the narrow party prejudices lying behind such slogans as 'progress' and 'reason'.

Disraeli was partly creating his own myth in *Tancred*: the Holborn lawyer's clerk was claiming membership of a spiritual aristocracy more ancient and more potent than any known to northern Europe. But he was also creating the most damning criticism of himself ever written: the Emir Fakredeen. This is the least discussed aspect of the novel, but perhaps the most curious.

Fakredeen, an engaging, 'fatally frank', charming villain, is the Vivian Grey of the East, a Levantine supercad, a compulsive intriguer and weaver of far-fetched combinations. He is wholly amoral, convinced that all is 'a matter of force or fraud' (*T* 214). He is, in short, one side of Disraeli, or Disraeli as much of the world saw him. He

possessed all the qualities of the genuine Syrian character in excess; vain, susceptible, endowed with a brilliant though frothy imagination, and a love of action so unrestrained that restlessness deprived it of energy, with so fine a taste that he was always capricious, and so ingenious that he seemed ever inconsistent. His ambition was as high as his apprehension was quick. He saw everything and understood everybody in a flash; and believed that everything that was said or done ought to be made to contribute to his fortunes . . . Stratagems came to him as naturally as fruit comes to a tree. (*T* 214.)

It is a sketch of a political magician. Disraeli knew only one such person. His purpose as an author in condemning himself was to make clear that the intriguer, as a type, is an ass, failing to achieve even his own low ends. Tancred loftily, and perhaps authorially, reflects: 'I do not believe anything great is ever affected by management.' (*T* 258.) Fakredeen's fatuous implausibility is illustrated by his plan for Queen Victoria 'to transfer the seat of her empire from London to Delhi' (*T* 263). Fakredeen is Disraeli sitting in judgement on himself, and finding himself wanting; and the remorseless self-analysis (*T* 213–15) is what Peel should have pronounced upon Disraeli had Peel been a Disraeli. The fall of Peel, that result of low stratagem, echoes in this tale of Lebanese intrigue.

Monypenny is right in his observation that 'Tancred strikes the reader less as the accomplishment of a political purpose, than as a sudden revolt of the author against the routine and hollowness of politics, against its prejudice and narrowness; and as an assertion of his detachment and superiority to it all by the glorification of his race' (M & B iii. 34). There may have been a change of mood in mid-novel; the first section was written in the autumn of 1845, when Disraeli had no political prospects, and the second in the latter part of 1846, when he had become a celebrated parliamentary leader. Even so, it belongs to a trilogy that is critical of English society; and *Tancred*, whether set in England or abroad, is a genuinely dissident voice protesting courageously against conventional pieties.

Not all of *Tancred* is exotic. The first third of it, set in England, reaffirmed a good deal of what had appeared in *Coningsby* and *Sybil*. Liberal modernity is here to stay; nothing much can be done about it, but then, not much needs to be done. 'Change, "in the abstract", is what is wanted by a people who are at the same time inquiring and wealthy.' (*T* 73.) All sections of the Church are airily dismissed: strange talk for a Tory, yet Disraeli manages to be offensive about High Church, Low Church, and Broad Church all in the same novel. For good measure he lambasts Irish Protestantism, dear to Tory hearts, as 'a Church that had from the first betrayed its trust' (*T* 69), repeating an enmity previously expressed in *Coningsby*. The Church of Dr Pusey, Lord Shaftesbury, and Bishop Blomfield was to Disraeli an empty vessel, a Sunday edition of Peelite conservatism or Lord Liverpool's mediocrity (a charge made both in *Coningsby* and *Tancred*).

The aristocracy, then, existed on sufferance, without spiritual support, presiding over the dissolution of traditional society. 'The people of this country have ceased to be a nation. They are a crowd, and only kept in some rude provisional discipline by the remains of that old system which they are daily destroying.' (*T* 51.) This distinction between crowd and community, which is also made in *Sybil*, is symbolized by Tancred's coming-of-age festivities on a great landed estate. These celebrate social cohesion in a stable moral order; they are the liturgy of Conservatism, and, as such, Disraeli returned to them in *Lothair*. Disintegration, Disraeli shows, is endemic even within high society itself. While one great lady of spiritual views speculates wildly in railway shares, another talks Tancred dead with her sub-scientific rationalism. 'You know, all is development', says the fair chatterer, until Tancred retorts: 'I do not believe I ever was a fish.' The Darwinian tide was washing through Disraeli's drawing-rooms twelve years before Darwin, showing that the latter was more consequence than cause.

Disraeli made two constructive suggestions in *Tancred:* no nation could hope for great architecture unless it first hanged an architect (*T* 122); and, 'if anything can save the aristocracy in this levelling age, it is an appreciation of the work of men of genius' (*T* 39)—though admittedly he was speaking here of a chef.

8 The Later Novels

THE novels *Lothair* (1870) and *Endymion* (1880) are sometimes seen as entertainments, if only because they entertain. They are relaxed; they glitter with knowledge of the great world; they propose no overt doctrine. True enough: they are poetry, a lyrical celebration of the innocence of wealth enclosed in a stable and confident moral order where all is accustomed, ceremonious. Yet such a display of the aristocratic virtues is itself a point of view, a hidden doctrine. Middle-class critics were little pleased by the comparison in *Lothair* between aristocratic serenity, bourgeois anxiety, and priestly worldliness. It is the aristocrat who rises above the deformities of the world, because his function is to *be* rather than to *do*; and yet, by only being, he performs a vital public office in the national life.

The justification of a social class in terms of a sub-Christian spirituality is a risky business; but if Disraeli's fictional aristocracy had less knowledge of the argument of force than in the 1840s, that was because the social landscape had changed. Bathed in popularity, ruling by consent with skill and enjoyment, with fortunes undiluted by plutocracy and undiminished by agricultural depression, the members of the aristocracy were not aware of the economic euthanasia that awaited them. They ruled the freest, richest, most successful nation the world had ever seen; no other class even wished to replace them. Well might they preside over national energy and social repose with guiltless minds. Guiltless, but not untroubled. The question facing a young man of the 1860s was what to believe. Young Lothair, orphaned at an early age, brought up without schooling or companions by a grim Scottish guardian, is just down from Oxford, the heir to great estates. He is a *tabula rasa* for the ideological tumults of the age.

One guardian was a Scottish Calvinist, but the other was a cardinal, not unlike Manning, who had gone over to Gladstone in 1868. Cardinal Grandison in *Lothair* was Disraeli's revenge: a flattering one. On one level, *Lothair* is a no-popery romance, a *Maria Monk* of the upper classes. But Disraeli says more than that Romanism is wily and prelatical and stops at nothing; he adds a weightier argument. The difference between Anglicanism and Romanism was not theological but social. Church and the social order are intimately linked; for a young noble who joined Rome prevented himself from being a natural leader of the nation, thus exposing it to government by unnatural ones. Old Roman Catholic families like the St Jeromes are portrayed as pious and aesthetically pleasing, but they cannot stand in the same relation to the nation as Anglicans, and hence their virtues are merely private ones. In choosing Rome, a young landowner is choosing not to exercise his public function.

Disraeli's point was a fair one. Romanism did in fact bring exclusion from public life. Young noblemen were at risk: Lord Bute's spectacular reception into the Roman Church in 1868 served as the model for Lothair. Disraeli had no petty sectarian or theological objections to the Roman faith, but his opposition to acts of abdication by the aristocracy was based on a belief that to separate religion from authority led to barbarism. 'The connexion of religion with the exercise of political authority is one of the main safeguards of the civilisation of man.'

The wiles of Rome were only one theme in *Lothair*. There was also the question of which woman was to guide Lothair's path. Lady Corisande, a tender if insipid English rose and a duke's daughter to boot, is first in the field, and, indeed, wins the race in the last furlong. In between, however, she is mainly conspicuous for her forgettability. The second candidate is the nun-like Catholic of an old family who wants Lothair to build Westminster Cathedral. She inspires slightly more respect; but it is Theodora who steals the show. Theodora is a principled revolutionary. She has more in common with the school of Mazzini than of Marx. She is an Italian dedicated to the liberation of Italy. She is a pure, lofty soul, albeit married to an American colonel—an arrangement which did not impede Lothair's adulation of her, for this is no fleshly tale. In real life Theodora was Mrs Jessie White, an Englishwoman who nursed on the battlefields of Italy with Garibaldi. Theodora is conscience without tradition, conscience unshaped by a moral order. She represents modernity, missionariness, the aspiration to regenerate society, and intensity. Her role is to *do*, not to *be*. She symbolizes, perhaps even heads, the forces of change in Europe. She is revolution placed on a pedestal, and found wanting.

For Disraeli, the attractiveness of the revolutionary is his or her goodness; and it is this goodness that must be guarded against. The seasoned revolutionary general, Captain Bruges, appears in *Lothair* as the perfect gentleman. Disraeli had only contempt for pretenders at revolution; of the Irish, Bruges says: 'No real business in them. Their treason is a fairy tale, and their sedition a child talking in its sleep.' The First International is likewise caricatured as the Standing Committee of the Holy Alliance of Peoples: a pot-house talking-shop relishing the rhetoric of extremism. It is the real revolutionary who is serious and good—and should be opposed, because his seriousness and goodness need to live through action.

Disraeli had several reasons for setting up Theodora in order to knock her down. First, he was the Tory leader; he had boycotted Garibaldi's visit to England. Secondly, his nervous temperament, always delicate, produced an exceptional, if intermittent, need for tranquillity which led him to idealize the rural peace of ducal life, sometimes absurdly. When Lady Corisande and her sisters 'asked their pretty questions and made their sparkling remarks, roses seemed to drop from their lips, and sometimes diamonds' (*L* 7).

Disraeli knew well enough that his novels bowdlerized the life of polite society, as his memoirs and letters show.

Nobody knew better the dark under-side of high society, or realized how much could not be mentioned in a Victorian novel. His conclusion is none the less what he really felt: that the harmonious torpor of a great landed estate, symbolized by the festivities at Lothair's coming-of-age, where all classes met on a basis of mutual affection and trust, was morally richer and less ambiguous than anything that exertion or merit could supply. Where there is no action, no whiff of the morally imperative, conflict can hardly arise. The message of *Lothair* is that great Victorian theme, the union of hearts in the context of rural and aristocratic values. Modernity is firmly rejected, even in its most attractive form—Theodora; and social optimism is firmly tied to traditionalism.

The critics could not see this. They could not forgive the absence of an elevated tone, by which they meant liberal high-mindedness. What were the author's principles? None that any liberal could see; worse, did not Disraeli mock the very idea of principle? As the young Henry James said, the critics were 'savagely negative'. At worst, they said, *Lothair* is two novels arbitrarily joined: a social comedy of English high society (pp. 1–275), switching without apology to Mediterranean melodrama (pp. 276–485). At best, they said, *Lothair* is valuable for its vignettes. The good things in it are its asides.

Disraeli did indeed make some happy inventions. He invented that Wodehousian figure, the glumly tyrannical head gardener (*L* ch. 13). He invented Tory anti-intellectualism with his portrait of the Oxford professor 'who was not satisfied with a home career', and whose 'restless vanity ... prevented him from ever observing or thinking of anything but himself'. 'Like sedentary men of extreme opinions, he was a social parasite.' (*L* ch. 24.) Here Baldwin was to continue what Disraeli had begun. Mr Phoebus (drawn from Lord Leighton) happily embodies the frailties of the artistic poseur. Through him, the Oxford professor, and a gallery of revolutionary types, the inadequacies of art, science, and revolution are successively exposed, and, after a few wise authorial words on race and religion from the oriental sage Paraclete, we are free to return to the redeeming virtues of the English landowner. The vignettes are not just vignettes: they are there to lead us to an irresistible conclusion.

Criticism of Lothair himself is misplaced. To Sir Leslie Stephen, the hero was 'a passive bucket to be poured into ... he is unpleasantly like a fool'. To which one may reply that an Oxford undergraduate, an orphan brought up in solitude, and not a public-school man, may well enter society in undecided mood. The verdict of Stephen, an agnostic Puritan and morose Alpinist, on *Lothair* was characteristically grim: 'a practical joke on a large scale, or a prolonged burlesque'. This perhaps tells us more about Stephen than about Disraeli; and in the twentieth century, when Alton Towers and Trentham, the homes of Lothair and Lady Corisande, form theme parks for the delight of the masses, it is Stephen's earnestness which has faded, and Disraeli's taste for magnificent settings which commands popular enthusiasm.

Politically, *Lothair* did Disraeli no good. Liberals thought it flash, vulgar, and lacking in seriousness; Tories were uneasily reminded that Disraeli was an alien being who kept losing them elections. Commercially, however, it was his most successful novel to date, reaching eight British editions in 1870. By the end of 1876 he had received £6,000 from *Lothair*. In America, 15,000 copies were sold on the first day. Financially, Disraeli's ship had come home at last.

Endymion, published in 1880, after Disraeli had lost office, received a publisher's advance of £10,000, the largest of its time. This was not undeserved. If its mood was serenely autumnal, it was not marked by fading power. Two or three of its best passages have passed into the language. Unlike its two predecessors, *Tancred* and *Lothair*, it was not marred by large areas of silliness. What other ex-Prime Minister (Disraeli was then 75) could have produced so happy a work of imagination just before his death? The tone is youthful. The novel not only ends with wedding bells; they intrude regularly into the narrative. Set in English political society between 1827 and 1855, the novel need not be taken as more than light entertainment.

The hero, Endymion, a youth of gentle birth (and not much else) is more of an author's dummy than Lothair. He does not ascend; he is elevated to fulfil the surrogate ambition of those around him. Forced by reduced circumstances to enter life as a government clerk, he is nevertheless raised to the premiership by the determination of his well-wishers. The chief among these is his twin sister, who first enters the Rothschild household as a companion to their daughter, then marries Palmerston, and then, on his death, marries Napoleon III (all, of course, in fictional guise). If that were not enough, another female well-wisher anonymously sends him £20,000 in order that he should have the means to enter Parliament. Truly, we are in fairyland.

The charm of the book, and it is as charming as it is mellow, lies in its sense of period, its grasp of history, and its vignettes of famous persons. Palmerston, Cobden, Manning, Napoleon III, and Bismarck are charitably portrayed; only Thackeray, seen as the most self-centred of social climbers, is harshly mocked. If little is usually said about *Endymion*, it is because it seems so self-explanatory. To most readers it is a story pure and simple, without a message and untouched by thought. It is a political novel without a political revelation; it is indeed a novel about politicians in which politics plays a minimal part, save for shifting the action from one scene to the next.

There is some casual repetition of earlier ideas. Secret societies still rule Europe; women still rule politics; race is the key to history; will overcomes all difficulties; and the Rothschilds, all-wise, are the spiders at the centre of the web. Such views were nothing new; but in *Endymion* Disraeli does not press or develop them. He had recanted nothing: so much is clear. If he had a new point to make, it was that tact and persuasiveness are the supreme political qualities. But *Endymion* is not a political novel; it is a society novel. Even more than *Lothair*, it is a study of London society, in the sense of the 'upper ten thousand'. It is in society, Disraeli asserts, that the alliances are made which determine careers. Parliament, by comparison with society, is a shadowy epiphenomenon. In quiet times it is society which makes up the political nation. Those outside London are outside society, and therefore outside politics. Society is St James's, Mayfair, and perhaps even South Kensington, and the country houses that go therewith. It is true, as Disraeli says, that should 'some event suddenly occur which makes a nation feel or think', then 'the whole thing might vanish like a dream'; but barring that, society goes its own way. The adventurer on the lowest rung of society counts for more, and has more opportunities, than the most notable figure (like Dickens) outside society. Society is the real hero of *Endymion*; of all great forces it is the most neglected by students of politics today or yesterday, because they stand outside it and are unaware of its operations.

Endymion is about 'the art of creating a career' (Schw. 142). Those who create careers are the women: ambitious, virile, ruthless women who wish to make things happen. Rich, powerful, and underemployed, they fulfil themselves by using groups of friends as instruments for determining the fortunes of the next generation. The group of friends, an artificial extended family, is the unit which determines advancement. Sociology, too used to painting with a broad brush, has been so concerned with the character of ruling classes as a whole that it has paid scant attention to the microsociology of advancement: how do individuals get to the top? To Disraeli this was a question of no small interest. His answer was that the advancement of individuals over a lifetime depends on multiple extreme improbabilities. Many of these improbabilities are social: a weekend matters more than a committee, a dinner more than a speech. Society, remarks Schwarz, is like the City or Parliament: a great self-regulating entity, the guarantor of its own health. In the end, its judgement is just; it does not make mistakes.

To those within society, little outside is visible. Though *Endymion* covers the same period as *Sybil*, the condition of England question is notable by its absence, save for one visit to the North. No social doctrine is suggested. Yet in the end there is a contradiction at the heart of *Endymion*. On the one hand Disraeli states that what matters is the world of those who do not work. This was no doubt as true in the 1870s as in the 1830s. On the other hand, *Endymion* is a 'bourgeois novel about succeeding in an aristocratic world' (Schw. 146). Like Samuel Smiles, though in a very different context, Disraeli sings the praises of honest toil; he has embraced Victorian values. Those who work, rise in the world. Lord Roehampton (Palmerston) embodies the aristocratic virtues; but in fact he is a workaholic who dies at his desk in the small hours. Job Thornberry (Cobden) and Nigel Penruddock (Manning) rise from humble origins to national greatness: their secret is application. That arduous toiler, Mrs Guy Flouncey, the great social climber of *Coningsby* and *Tancred*, had once been the exception; now, in 1880, her disciplined approach to social success has become the rule. Even Endymion's own ascent, though forged for him by others, could not have been sustained without dull tenacity on his part. Work may even gain a throne, as with Napoleon III, or an authority exceeding that of mere governments, such as Neuchatel (Rothschild) possesses. In *Endymion* all those who succeed, work (including, not least, the great ladies); and upward mobility is there for all who honestly seek it.

Two eras mingle in *Endymion*. The Disraeli of 1880 dwells fondly on the Disraeli of the 1830s, the pet of great ladies; but his eye also falls on a gallery of eminent Victorians who made their own destiny. Young Endymion, who is Disraeli without the genius, is the toy of a benevolent establishment which open-mindedly looks after whatever it comes to see as its own.

9 Interpretations and Comparisons

Is there controversy about the interpretation of Disraeli? The answer is that there is more than there was ten years ago; that there is less, much less, than there is about Gladstone; that the area of controversy is gradually widening, after a long post-war consensus on Disraeli; and that while in the Harold Wilson era it was natural for academics to stress similarities with Wilson, today they are readier to see him as, in part, a 'conviction politician'; though what those convictions are, is itself in dispute.

Lord Blake's classic biography, *Disraeli* (1966) (especially pp. 757–766), provided the first full-scale interpretation. It remained alone in the field for a long time, simply because all the major studies of particular episodes in Disraeli's career have been in tune with it or appeared to confirm its views. M. Cowling and F. B. Smith on the Second Reform act; Paul Smith on Disraelian social reform; Richard Millman on Disraeli's foreign policy; Robert Stewart on protectionism; and the published diaries of Lord Stanley—these all stressed the autonomy of Disraeli's political practice. Disraeli, they say, may have had broad principles (English greatness, and aristocratic rule in some mildly updated form), but these did not determine his practice in particular cases. He also had personal principles: the prudence of forgiveness, for example. He was not, in a derogatory sense, a man of no principle; but his principles did not explain his actions.

This 'opportunist' view of Disraeli was all to the good, in that it turned its back on a naïve Anglo-Saxon moralism that assumed politicians had 'principles' of which their careers were the outward embodiment. It also recognized that party leaders who act without an eye to the main chance do not last long. It drew particularly on an examination of Disraeli's footwork in times of crisis, as over reform in

1867, or over the Eastern question in 1876–8. Indeed, on the immediate question of what Disraeli did in these cases, we disagree surprisingly little; perhaps less than we should if we currently surveyed his attitudes over the decades. The opportunist view of Disraeli was not political, in that the same conclusions were reached irrespective of the party ties, or even the nationality, of the writer. Disraeli, all were agreed, was a remarkable human being, perhaps an admirable one; but not admirable in the crude way in which speakers at Tory conferences thought he was admirable. Blake saved Disraeli for all time from a reputation as a Tory plaster saint. The opportunist view cannot be wrong, for Disraeli was blatantly opportunist. The question that has been raised recently is whether it is wholly right or only partially so.

In an article published in 1984, P. R. Ghosh pays particular attention to Disraeli's views on public finance. Rightly, he says this aspect has been neglected; Disraeli was after all Chancellor of the Exchequer three times. Ghosh says that in this field Disraeli did have principles, and that they did closely affect his actions; but they were basically the same as everybody else's principles: namely (broadly speaking), those of a Peelite, peace-loving, and economical Little Englander. Thus, to Ghosh, Disraeli was a 'sincere' exponent of the mid-Victorian consensus: peace, retrenchment, and reform, embellished with social unity (though not with collectivism), and tied together with a pacific foreign policy which kept defence costs, and thus taxes, down. Disraeli also aimed to integrate the landed interest and agriculture within an urban society, on essentially urban terms. So Disraeli in his middle period was all but a Tory Gladstone—and not solely from necessity, but because he believed it. Ghosh believes that both Disraeli's middle period (1849–68) and his policies (especially outside the crises) have been underexamined. Were we to make good this deficiency, we would see the essential Disraeli in the Chancellor who wore the mantle of Peel, not in the 'tired and passive premier' of 1874–80, wearing the mantle of Palmerston.

A third view is that put forward in an article by Paul Smith, published in 1987. Smith, unlike Ghosh and Blake, stresses the unity of Disraeli's life; the importance of his Jewishness; the irrelevance of the question: was Disraeli sincere?; and the centrality of his ideas. These, says Smith, cannot be 'swept aside as a mere bag of burglar's tools' for breaking and entering the British establishment. It was through his ideas, says Smith, that Disraeli created a parallel personal and political identity which was comparable in its way to the creation of a work of art.

This raises many questions. The first is that of Jewishness. Lord Blake had not dwelt over-much on this, preferring to see Disraeli as part stage-Italian, part product of a very distinctive pre-Victorian generation. (Disraeli's drawing-room incongruously contained portraits of Byron, Lady Blessington, Count D'Orsay, and Queen Victoria.) The difficulty here is that while there is enough evidence to create a mystery about Disraeli's Jewish dimension, there is not enough to solve it. The second question is that of the unity of Disraeli's ideas over a lifetime. This is partly linked to the question of Jewishness, for if that were a constant preoccupation, it greatly strengthens the case for his being a man of coherent outlook. Smith, while conceding that Disraeli's ideas 'are nothing like a system of political philosophy', describes them as 'a more extensive and coherent set of observations on English history, character, and destiny than has yet been exposed to public view by almost any other party leader'. The key question, for Smith, is not Disraeli's sincerity, but how he created an identity, and what he used it for.

This differs in focus from Lord Blake's more political judgement that Disraeli's early ideas and later practice belong to different worlds. 'The truth is', writes Blake, 'that Disraeli had principles when he led the party and believed in them sincerely, but they were not the "principles", if that word can be used at all, of Young England.' (B 761–3.) For Blake, the crucial break in Disraeli's public career came with Palmerston's death in 1865. Before then Disraeli could not wear the mantle of Palmerston; indeed, given the rules of adversarial politics, he had to go through the motions of opposing Palmerston's John Bullishness. Perhaps Disraeli had a wider range of identities, and a more flexible one, than is generally recognized. He looked to national consensus in the 1830s and again in the 1870s; it does not follow that the intermediate decades were consistent. In the 1840s, Young England was more about social cohesion than national identity. In 1855–65 Disraeli was reduced to seeking any position that was not occupied by Palmerston, which meant creating his 'church' identity, an underrated aspect of his career. It was only in the 1870s that the two themes of social cohesion and national identity were finally integrated.

Still, endings do matter; and the ending of the 1870s owed much to Disraeli's ideas of the 1830s. And what was an ending for Disraeli, was for English Conservatism the beginning of a largely successful century managed on broadly Disraelian lines. An adversarial party system probably has room for only one party of national identity at a time—meaning English national identity, and leaving Scotland, Ireland, and perhaps Wales out of it, as aspects of the un-Englishness of the opposition. This began as an anti-O'Connell tactic in the 1830s; generalized, it became a stable component of political culture. It was a close-run thing for the Tories. They did not necessarily have to end up as the party uniting—or appearing to unite—social cohesion and national identity. Palmerston nearly appropriated the latter, while Gladstone made a good try at making social cohesion the Liberal trade mark. Many Conservative parties elsewhere failed to make the crucial move from élite parties to mass parties, partly because they did not have a brand image, or not one that could be put across in popular terms. It is to Disraeli's mental footwork as much as anything that the Conservatives owe their survival.

Disraeli's climb 'to the top of the greasy pole', as he called it, is itself an interpretation of his life, and an important one, especially at a popular level. The supposedly unique improbability of his becoming Prime Minister becomes more important than anything he did: a sensation of wonder is supposed to replace all else. This will not do. In any generation, then or now, the odds against any individual becoming Prime Minister are no doubt enormous. But taken a stage at a time instead of in one huge leap—taken, that is, as it happened in real life—each transition becomes less remarkable. For the talented heir to a Chiltern estate to enter Parliament (not easily, perhaps, but after great persistence) was neither unexpected nor a mark of genius; for that talented MP, after a long interval, to make his mark in a crisis not of his choosing; for him to colonize a faction of back-benchers bereft of talent; for him to be marked out by Derby as an essential subordinate—none of these elevations presents any puzzle. The most unlikely step of all was perhaps the last. Had Derby retired somewhat earlier or somewhat later, in the immediate shadow of the 1865 defeat or just after the 1868 débâcle, then the party would have gone to all lengths to avoid a Disraeli premiership.

In fact, Disraeli's Cabinet was socially a mixed bag. The Lord Chancellor, Lord Cairns, was a middle-class Belfast lawyer who lived in a villa in Bournemouth. Gathorne Hardy was a Bradford industrialist and lawyer: business money with some rural pretensions. Cross was a banker; W. H. Smith ran W. H. Smith's. Northcote was a squire, but he was not a grand figure—more of an Oxford meritocrat. Ward Hunt and Pakington were only country gentlemen by the accident of unexpected inheritance. The surprise is not that the Tories drew on men without great social position, but that the historic families could produce a Derby and a Salisbury capable of leading with true distinction. In any case, the Disraeli who became Prime Minister was no Vivian Grey, but had been a central figure in the highest society for over twenty years. The idea of Disraeli the miraculous outsider does not quite stand up.

How does Disraeli compare with others in thought and politics? Most obviously, he was (like Gladstone) a social optimist. Unlike Salisbury, the other great Conservative thinker, he was not haunted by fear of the masses. However complex his tactics in 1867, he trusted the people at least as much as he trusted anyone. Where Carlyle had despaired of an industrial society based on the cash nexus, Disraeli thought the answer to industrialism was strong, semi-feudal business leadership. Lord Quinton was right to see him as an optimist—about democracy, about urbanization, about England as a happy and united family. Disraeli was also a great Conservative sceptic. He disbelieved not merely the arguments, but even the very vocabulary, of conventional political discussion. 'The truth is, progress and reaction are but words to mystify the millions. They mean nothing, they are nothing, they are phrases and not facts.' (*LGB* 239.) The splendid spectacle of English freedom is just that: spectacle. Disraeli rejected the fetishism of words in politics, as Marx and Namier rejected similar idolatries in economics and history. In this he was far more radical than the radicals.

As a social thinker, Disraeli was before his time. Without using modern vocabulary, he often referred to the standard contrast between 'crowd' and 'community'; to the element of 'social control' involved in apparently liberal institutions and (still more) values; and to the way in which mass politics would require the charismatic individual. 'Great minds must trust to great truths and great talents for their rise, and nothing else.' (*C* 58). In an author prone to charlatanism, it is especially important to remember that in an experimental way he foreshadows central elements in modern social thought.

Disraeli did not believe that there was an admirable abstraction called Conservatism. He accepted party as reality, but remained emotionally detached. 'Yes', he told an intimate in 1850, 'we are both on the wrong side, but there is nothing for it but to make the best of it.' Had the patronage of Lord Durham in the 1830s or Palmerston in the 1840s come his way as sought, there was no reason why Disraeli should not have become an effective Liberal politician without any liberal illusions. After all, as he told Derby proudly in 1849, 'I am Disraeli, the adventurer.'

Disraeli's unrestrained delight in aristocracy was aesthetic, not political. It was partly a matter of landscape, not least his obsession with cool woodland. It was partly, too, a way of writing about the idealized youthful male: very youthful on the whole, except for Egremont, the hero of *Sybil*, who is a veteran of 30 or so. The emotional focus is on life before 21, reflecting the youth Disraeli hardly had; and the distinction Disraeli drew between the artless boy of 20 and the tired old man of 25, mortally sick with boredom, was sharp indeed. Disraeli's doctrine of aristocracy grew out of a doctrine of the ideal boyhood, conveyed in the only readable passage in *The Revolutionary Epick* (1864 edn., pp. 41–2):

> He who is bred
> Within an honoured place, and from the womb
> Unto his grave nought sordid views; but taught
> By all the glories of his ancestors
> Them to remember, does himself respect:
> Around whose infant image all men's thoughts
> Cluster with hope; who mixing with the crowd
> Feels like a trophy in the market-place
> He is their own: who from his lofty state,
> As from some tower, the social regions views
> Unclouded by the vapour or the vale
> Bounding a vulgar vision, but intent
> To make the Law more loved, the leisure gives
> That Law hath given to him; who chases wisdom
> Within her treasured coverts: keen his sport
> O'er what he finds deep musing; or to talk
> With scholar ripe or brainful traveller
> May love, and artist in his drooping hour:
> This man, thus honoured, set apart, refined,
> Serene and courteous, learned, thoughtful, brave,
> As full of charity as noble pomp,
> Pledge in the tempests of the world, the stream
> Of culture shall not ebb: the Noble this
> Mankind demands, and Nations love to trust.

Conservatism is often portrayed as having two poles, with Disraeli at one end and Margaret Thatcher at the other. This is hardly correct. It is usually taken to mean that Disraeli saw collectivism, or the big state, as the natural embodiment of social cohesion and national unity. That is certainly incorrect. Disraeli did not look forward to the welfare state; as P. R. Ghosh points out, in 1873 Disraeli pronounced that, 'All the questions of Trade and Navigation, of the Incidence of Taxation and of Public Economy are settled.' This was not the language of a man who foresaw, or would have welcomed, the century of anti-individualism between 1880 and 1980. Indeed, there are certain resemblances between the two leaders. Both had a long period of political dormancy. Both, despite that, had a fundamental unity of outlook throughout their long careers. Both sought to replace one firmly rooted consensus with another. Both, to some degree, succeeded. Both faced the greatest pressure experienced by a Prime Minister in fifty years: Disraeli in 1876; Margaret Thatcher in 1981. Both responded by intensifying their policies. Both disregarded those narrow prejudices Lord Blake describes as 'the moral anxieties of the prosperous intelligentsia'; both were correct in seeing the articulate classes as marginal. Both originated in, and continued to identify with, groups outside gentry Conservatism. Both upheld economic liberalism as the rule in public life, while implying that other values should apply in private life. Both preferred the appearance of strength to the reality in defence and international matters.

The resemblance is confined to public affairs. 'Always stick to Irony: there you are safe' (F 428), was Disraeli's maxim; and because of this, the inner Disraeli can only rarely be glimpsed.

Further Reading

Of the many lives of Disraeli, two in particular stand out: *Disraeli* by Robert Blake, now Lord Blake (Eyre and Spottiswoode, 1966), perhaps the best biography of a Victorian figure; and the authorized life in six volumes by W. F. Monypenny and G. E. Buckle, *The Life of Benjamin Disraeli, Earl of Beaconsfield* (Murray, 1910–20), which is partisan but well-documented. By comparison, Disraeli's own attempt at autobiography, centring on his early life, is slender if evocative: see *Disraeli's Reminiscences*, ed. Helen M. Swartz and Marvin Swartz (Macmillan, 1975).

Accessibility, among other good reasons, has led most readers to approach Disraeli's novels through the two best-known works, *Coningsby* and *Sybil*. Both are available in paperback in The World's Classics (OUP 1982 and 1981 respectively), ed. Dr Sheila M. Smith, an authority on Disraeli's fictional methods.

Disraeli's political theory is largely collected under the posthumous title, *Whigs and Whiggism: Political Writings by Benjamin Disraeli*, ed. and introd. William Hutcheon (Murray, 1913). On the Jewish aspect, see Cecil Roth, *Benjamin Disraeli, Earl of Beaconsfield* (The Philosophical Library, 1952).

For Disraeli's ideas on race, see D. L. Dinkin's comprehensive study, 'The Racial and Political Ideas of Benjamin Disraeli', M.Sc. thesis (Bristol, 1980).

There is much on Disraeli as a political craftsman. On reform, see F. B. Smith, *The Making of the Second Reform Bill* (CUP, 1966), and M. Cowling, *1867, Disraeli, Gladstone and Revolution: The Passing of the Second Reform Bill* (CUP, 1967). On party organization, E. J. Feuchtwanger's *Disraeli, Democracy and the Tory Party: Conservative Leadership and Organization after the Second Reform Bill* (OUP, 1968), is essential. For a close-up picture over a long period, see *Disraeli, Derby, and the Conservative Party: Journals and Memoirs of Edward Henry, Lord Stanley, 1849–1869*, ed. John Vincent (Harvester, 1978). On foreign policy, see especially R. W. Seton–Watson, *Disraeli, Gladstone and the Eastern Question: A Study in Diplomacy and Politics* (Macmillan, 1935), and Richard Millman, *Britain and the Eastern Question 1875–1878* (OUP, 1979). On empire, see C. C. Eldridge, *England's*

Further Reading

Mission: The Imperial Idea in the Age of Gladstone and Disraeli, 1868–1880 (Macmillan, 1973). On Disraeli's social policy, the key work is Paul Smith's *Disraelian Conservatism and Social Reform* (Routledge, 1967).

For Disraeli's youth, the fullest study is B. R. Jerman's *The Young Disraeli* (Princeton, 1960). His early travels are covered in *Benjamin Disraeli in Spain, Malta, and Albania, 1830–32: A Monograph*, by Donald Sultana (new and enlarged edn.; Tamesis, 1976), and by Lord Blake in *Disraeli's Grand Tour: Benjamin Disraeli and the Holy Land, 1830–31* (Weidenfeld, 1982).

For contemporary views of Disraeli, see P. W. Clayden (a Liberal activist), *England under Lord Beaconsfield: The Political History of Six Years from the End of 1873 to the Beginning of 1880* (Kegan Paul, 1880); *The Journals of Lady Knightley of Fawsley, 1856–1884*, ed. Julia Cartwright (Murray, 1915); and Sir William Augustus Fraser, *Disraeli and his Day* (Kegan Paul, 1891), all of which provide interesting perspectives, the latter two from a Tory back-bench angle.

For Disraeli's early leadership, see Robert Mackenzie Stewart, *The Politics of Protection: Lord Derby and the Protectionist Party, 1841–1852* (CUP, 1971); and, more broadly, his *The Foundation of the Conservative Party* (Longman, 1976), Lord Blake's *The Conservative Party from Peel to Thatcher* (Methuen, 1985), and Bruce Coleman's *Conservatism and the Conservative Party in Nineteenth-Century Britain* (Edward Arnold, 1988).

Numerous literary critics have discussed Disraeli's fiction. For a powerful psychological interpretation, see Daniel R. Schwarz, *Disraeli's Fiction* (Macmillan, 1979). There is an authoritative bibliography by R. W. Stewart, *Benjamin Disraeli: A List of Writings by him, and Writings about him, with Notes* (The Scarecrow Press, 1972).

Disraeli's collected correspondence is being prepared for publication, four volumes having appeared to date (1989). See *Benjamin Disraeli: Letters*, vols. i (1815–34) and ii (1835–7) ed. J. A. W. Gunn, John Matthews, Donald M. Schurman, and M. G. Wiebe (University of Toronto Press, 1982); vols. iii (1838–41) and iv (1842–7), ed. M. G. Wiebe, J. B. Conacher, John Matthews, and Mary S. Millar (University of Toronto Press, 1987, 1989). Of several other selections from his correspondence, the most revealing is *The Letters of Disraeli to Lady Bradford and Lady Chesterfield*, ed. The Marquis of Zetland (Ernest Benn, 1929), 2 vols.

For personal interpretations of Disraeli, see Blake, *Disraeli*, pp. 757–66; P. R. Ghosh, 'Disraelian Conservatism: A Financial Approach', *English Historical Review*, 99 (1984), 268–96; P. R. Ghosh, 'Style and Substance in Disraelian Social Reform, *c*.1860–80', in *Politics and Social Change in Modern Britain: Essays Presented to A. F. Thompson*, ed. P. J. Waller (Harvester, 1987); J. Vincent 'Disraeli', in *The Prime Ministers*, ii, ed. H. Van Thal (Allen and Unwin, 1975), 85–108; J. Vincent, 'Was Disraeli A Failure?', *History Today*, 31 (Oct. 1981), 5–8; Anthony Quinton, *The Politics of Imperfection* (Faber, 1978), 79–84; Paul Smith, 'Disraeli's Politics', *Transactions of the Royal Historical Society*, 5th series, 37 (1987), 65–85.

Index

OXFORD

MORE OXFORD PAPERBACKS

Details of a selection of other Oxford Paperbacks follow. A complete list of Oxford Paperbacks, including The World's Classics, Twentieth-Century Classics, OPUS, Past Masters, Oxford Authors, Oxford Shakespeare, and Oxford Paperback Reference, is available in the UK from the General Publicity Department, Oxford University Press (RS), Walton Street, Oxford, OX2 6DP.

In the USA, complete lists are available from the Paperbacks Marketing Manager, Oxford University Press, 200 Madison Avenue, New York, NY 10016.

Oxford Paperbacks are available from all good bookshops. In case of difficulty, customers in the UK can order direct from Oxford University Press Bookshop, 116 High Street, Oxford, Freepost, OX1 4BR, enclosing full payment. Please add 10 per cent of the published price for postage and packing.

PAST MASTERS

General Editor: Keith Thomas

Past Masters is a series of authoritative studies that introduce students and general readers alike to the thought of leading intellectual figures of the past whose ideas still influence many aspects of modern life.

'This Oxford University Press series continues on its encyclopaedic way... One begins to wonder whether any intelligent person can afford not to possess the whole series.' *Expository Times*

KIERKEGAARD

Patrick Gardiner

Søren Kierkegaard (1813–55), one of the most original thinkers of the nineteenth century, wrote widely on religious, philosophical, and literary themes. But his idiosyncratic manner of presenting some of his leading ideas initially obscured their fundamental import.

This book shows how Kierkegaard developed his views in emphatic opposition to prevailing opinions, including certain metaphysical claims about the relation of thought to existence. It describes his reaction to the ethical and religious theories of Kant and Hegel, and it also contrasts his position with doctrines currently being advanced by men like Feuerbach and Marx. Kierkegaard's seminal diagnosis of the human condition, which emphasizes the significance of individual choice, has arguably been his most striking philosophical legacy, particularly for the growth of existentialism. Both that and his arresting but paradoxical conception of religious belief are critically discussed, Patrick Gardiner concluding this lucid introduction by indicating salient ways in which they have impinged on contemporary thought.

Also available in Past Masters: